THE 3:16 JOURNEY
A Discovery of Love

Kerrilee Burkhardt

Copyright © 2020 by Kerrilee Burkhardt
All rights reserved. This book or any portion thereof may not be reproduced or used in
any manner whatsoever without the express written permission of the publisher except
for the use of brief quotations in a book review.

"Scripture quotations taken from the New American Standard Bible® (NASB), Copyright © 1960, 1962, 1963, 1968, 1971, 1972, 1973, 1975, 1977, 1995 by The Lockman Foundation Used by permission. www.Lockman.org"
Scripture quotations marked (CEV) are from the Contemporary English Version Copyright © 1991, 1992, 1995 by American Bible Society. Used by Permission. The Holy Bible, English Standard Version® (ESV®) Copyright © 2001 by Crossway, a publishing ministry of Good News Publishers. All rights reserved. GOD'S WORD is a copyrighted work of God's Word to the Nations. Quotations are used by permission. Copyright 1995 by God's Word to the Nations. All rights reserved. Scripture quotations marked HCSB are been taken from the Holman Christian Standard Bible®, Copyright © 1999, 2000, 2002, 2003 by Holman Bible Publishers. Used by permission. Holman Christian Standard Bible®, Holman CSB®, and HCSB® are federally registered trademarks of Holman Bible Publishers.Scripture quotations marked (TLB) are taken from The Living Bible copyright © 1971. Used by permission of Tyndale House Publishers, a Division of Tyndale House Ministries, Carol Stream, Illinois 60188. All rights reserved. Scripture quotations marked MSG are taken from THE MESSAGE, copyright © 1993, 2002, 2018 by Eugene H. Peterson. Used by permission of NavPress. All rights reserved. Represented by Tyndale House Publishers, a Division of Tyndale House Ministries. "Scripture quotations taken from the New American Standard Bible® (NASB), Copyright © 1960, 1962, 1963, 1968, 1971, 1972, 1973, 1975, 1977, 1995 by The Lockman Foundation Used by permission. www.Lockman.org" Scripture quotation taken from the New Century Version®. Copyright © 2005 by Thomas Nelson. Used by permission. All rights reserved. NET Bible® copyright ©1996-2017 by Biblical Studies Press, L.L.C. http://netbible.com All rights reserved.; Scripture quotations marked (NIV) are taken from the Holy Bible, New International Version®, NIV®. Copyright © 1973, 1978, 1984, 2011 by Biblica, Inc.™ Used by permission of Zondervan. All rights reserved worldwide. www.zondervan.com The "NIV" and "New International Version" are trademarks registered in the United States Patent and Trademark Office by Biblica, Inc.™ New Life Version (NLV) Copyright © 1969, 2003 by Barbour Publishing, Inc.; Scripture quotations marked (NLT) are taken from the Holy Bible, New Living Translation, copyright ©1996, 2004, 2015 by Tyndale House Foundation. Used by permission of Tyndale House Publishers, a Division of Tyndale House Ministries, Carol Stream, Illinois 60188. All rights reserved.

First Printing, 2020
First Edition
HardtHouse Publishing
P.O Box 240 Buddina
Qld, Aus, 4575
www.hardthouse.com

Forward

Have you ever looked at a number and felt that there was something behind it? I don't believe in numerology or anything of that sort, but I have always been fascinated by numbers. And no, math is not my strong point at all. I mean, I am fascinated by a series of numbers. Like when you check your speedometer in the car and it says 13333.33 or 12345.67 or it seems that every time you look at a clock it is the same time. Or that a series of appointments, birthdays and so forth are all happening on the same date – regardless of the month.

Well this brings me to my 3:16 journey. I'm ashamed to admit it, but it took about two years for God to get through to me before I had the courage to listen and act. I believe God placed on my heart to write a devotional on every chapter 3 verse 16 in the Bible. I knew He was gently prodding me to do this, because everywhere I looked the numbers 3 and 16 were in my face. My heart truly believes that I have been asked to do this, so we can concrete our understanding of His love and purpose for our lives. I firmly believe this, even when the verses seem random and, well, when you check out some of them, harsh.

Maybe God chose 3:16 because of John 3:16, which, I'm pretty sure, is the most well-known verse in the Bible – the ultimate promise of Love. Maybe He wanted us to realise that He has a message throughout His Word; a theme.

I hope that this will bring you closer to knowing the Love of our Father and are a gentle reminder of what it is that He did for us. I have drawn so much closer to my precious Father since I started writing this book and I pray that there are some little snippets within here that resonate with you. I pray, too, that you can have your own falling-in-love-with-Jesus moments, too.

Please enjoy your 3:16 Journey – a discovery of Love.

Genesis 3:16
(TLB)

16 Then God said to the woman, "You shall bear children in intense pain and suffering; yet even so, you shall welcome your husband's affections, and he shall be your master."

At first glance, this verse is pretty disheartening. 'Oh, yay God, pain through childbirth, so much to look forward to! And I will want my husband, but he will rule over me! Huh! Why?'

We could then go off and moan about how mean and nasty God is. After all, what did *we* do wrong? We weren't Adam and Eve, we didn't eat the forbidden fruit. We are just a result of *their* stuff-up. How long must we suffer for their mistake?

I've been guilty of saying that, and, I'm sure, if you are honest with yourself, you've said something along those lines, too. It's all very easy to separate the Old Testament from today. It was so long ago – how could it possibly have relevance today?

I believe Genesis 3:16 is a reminder of what we threw away in our lust for power and control. It is also a reminder that, as long as we are here on Earth, there will always be a discord between man and woman. In contrary, in the garden there was complete peace and harmony.

So, how do we overcome this?

Well, in our own strength we can't.

This is where the love of Christ comes in. When, as man and woman, husband and wife, we focus our first love on Jesus, He, through His grace, will work on our behalf to help us to have a successful marriage. As long as we keep our eyes focused on God, our marriages can live in harmony. When we turn away from His love, that's when discord strikes and marriages fail.

In the garden, Eve chose to seek out power and control over her husband. Adam chose to follow his wife and ignore God's command. For their sin, they were punished. This is the way it is. God has never wavered, for it is said loud and clear,

Romans 6:23 (GWT) *'The payment for sin is death, but the gift that God freely gives is everlasting life found in Christ Jesus our Lord.'*

In short, God could have wiped out mankind in the garden. He didn't, but, as He cannot be untrue to Himself, we had to be punished. His love, though, is so great that He gave us another chance and He devoted the entire Holy Bible - His Word - to showing us how He will redeem us back to Himself.

Exodus 3:16
(NLT)

> 16"Now go and call together all the elders of Israel. Tell them, 'The LORD, the God of your ancestors - the God of Abraham, Isaac, and Jacob - has appeared to me. ~~He~~ told me, "I have been watching closely, and I see how the Egyptians are treating you."

These words are so powerful. I believe they are just as relevant today as they were in the time when Moses was called to free his people from Egypt.

We live in a world where there is so much pain and anguish and, in many parts of the world, calling yourself a follower of Christ can mean a death sentence. The Truth, though, is that nothing happens without God's okay. I know that this is tough, as we often wonder why He allows death, mayhem, murder, disease, heartbreak, famine and so on. Unfortunately, this is a side effect of His greatest gift – free will! We chose to shape the world we live in. We chose to move inch by inch away from the rules He put in place.

There are 10! That's it! 10 rules!

Most of us, if we are honest, like to *think* we live by at least some of these 10 Commandments. The 'don't murder' one, is pretty high up on the *Don't-do List*. Often our excuse for missing out on a few of these rules is that we want to believe that God has set the benchmark so high, that we can never reach it.

It is Man, however, who complicated things. It is Man who created his own set of rules that are so complex and unobtainable that they get lost in translation, so other men decide to create their own set of rules that are so complex and unobtainable that *they* get lost in translation and then other men decide to create... okay, you get the picture.

In Moses' day there were many, many rules, all of which were made up to help the powerful gain more and more control. Having an 'in' with a 'god' made you powerful. So, man created gods so that they felt superior and could be in control of their own little kingdoms. Making up rules to keep the people in slavery to the gods, was a way of power. Sadly, even men of the True Living God did the same.

God spoke to Moses and, in essence, said, 'I know what you are going through! I know that you have heard My voice and want to be obedient to Me, even though you have so many rules to follow, and you are struggling to hear My voice. I hear your pain and suffering. I see what is going on and I tell you here and now – I will do something about it.'

That has been God's way since the beginning – carrying us, His children, through the mess of our own making.

Wow!

That is love!

He never leaves us to get out of the mess alone. That is His constant throughout His Word. Never will I leave you!

See Hebrews 13:5, Deuteronomy 31:8 Josh 1:5.

His Word is His love story for you.

Leviticus 3:16
(NLT)

16and the priest will burn them on the altar. It is a special gift of food, a pleasing aroma to the LORD. All the fat belongs to the LORD.

Before Jesus came to Earth and became the ultimate sacrifice for all mankind, people of the Old Testament believed, and rightly so according to their custom and history, that a sacrifice of blood was needed to be made for the Lord God.

Interestingly, the first blood sacrifice happened in Genesis before the banishment of man from the garden.

Genesis 3:21(NLT) *And the LORD God made clothing from animal skins for Adam and his wife.*

How did God get the skin from the animal without shedding blood? Impossible – an animal became a sacrifice for man.

So in between the first blood sacrifice and the ultimate blood sacrifice of Jesus' crucifixion, man has been trying to bridge the divide between God and man. Of course, man cannot do this, only

God can.

The blood sacrifice is a reminder of God's love for man – He provided in the garden even when man sinned and He has provided for man every step of the way ever since. He ultimately showed His love for man when he gave His Son, as a pure and Holy sacrifice, for all mankind.

John 19:30 (NLT) *'It is finished'*. Meaning – He has done it all! Because He has loved us, mere mankind, no matter how much we have despised him, He made the ultimate sacrifice of blood so that we shall all live a life free of the burden of ritual.

If there is no need for sacrifice in today's world, what, then, is required of us to have a relationship with God?

Romans 10:9 (NASB) *that if you confess with your mouth Jesus as Lord, and believe in your heart that God raised Him from the dead, you will be saved.*

No more bloodshed in God's name – He has done it! Yes, it is finished indeed.

Numbers 3:16
(HCSB)

16So Moses registered them in obedience to the LORD as he had been commanded

The Book of Numbers is a slog – historians, economists and accountants might love the in-depth detail of the census of Numbers. For the rest of us, it can be tough to understand what is the purpose of this book, moreover, what is the significance of Numbers 3:16.

The book of Numbers is not only a census, it is a show of God's unfailing, unending love and patience for human short-comings. The people of Israel, just like you and me, complained and argued about everything.

Memories are short.

God led them out of Egypt, but that was *so yesterday*. We can easily look at the people in the Bible and say, "Gosh what a bunch of sooks, can't they see what God has done for them?!" This is where we need to look in the mirror and ask ourselves why we keep griping about how our lives are! The same God who led the Israelites out of the desert is the same God who is leading you out of yours.

We humans need order, we need someone to follow and, in short, we really do need someone to tell us what to do. If we are left to our own devices, we run-amuck.

The people of the book of Numbers needed a purpose. God wanted them to understand that His way was the only way and by following Him, He would lead them out of *their* desert and into the promised land. So, God gave them a purpose; something to keep their minds active and their hands from becoming idle.

The children of Levi were called to be counted – the first-born male from the age of one month.

One month old!

For they were called to serve the Lord, not to fight (other census counted first born males from 20 years old).

These children were born, not knowing where they would end up in their life – but God knew. He had a purpose for them, for His Glory.

A changing point in my life was when I read Rick Warren's book, *The Purpose Driven Life*. Chapter 2 – *You Are Not an Accident!*

To learn that God orchestrated my birth, and that of my children, set me free from the bondage of the choices I had made and the place I had allowed myself to get to. I was not a mistake; my children were not mistakes – **you** are not a mistake.

You are called to be counted, you are called to be the child of the living God. You have a purpose, there is a reason for you being here.

In Numbers 3:16 the first born were counted to serve the Lord. Today you are counted in the number of those who are called to serve the Lord.

Serve with your heart, your words, your hands, your love. Turn your eyes towards the King of Kings, Lord of Lords and know He has a purpose and a plan for your life.

Jeremiah 29:11 (NIV) *[11]For I know the plans I have for you," declares the Lord, "plans to prosper you and not to harm you, plans to give you hope and a future.*

It is an honour and a privileged to be called and counted by God. So, serve in His Kingdom, here on Earth, in our own little piece of this world that He has given to us, for His Glory.

Deuteronomy 3:16
(NIV)

16But to the Reubenites and the Gadites I gave the territory extending from Gilead down to the Arnon Gorge (the middle of the gorge being the border) and out to the Jabbok River, which is the border of the Ammonites.

Freedom! Ahh, how we love this word. Are any of us truly free though? When you think of freedom what does it mean to you?

I can do whatever I want, whenever I want?

No one telling me what to do, I make my own rules?

I tell others what to do, and I do it whenever, however and with whomever I please?

The dictionary describes it as *"the power or right to act, speak or think as one wants. Or the state of not being imprisoned or enslaved."*

So, which one is it? If we have the power or right to act, speak or think as we want – can't that very thing land us back in prison? Does this mean we must look deeper as to the meaning of freedom? Can we still be free while psychically imprisoned? Paul seems to believe this. He is cited on more than one occasion talking about what truly being free acually means.

Our 3:16 verse today was written about 1406BC at the end of the time of wandering in the desert – 40 years and even hundreds before that, the Israelites were prisoners. Here Moses is offering them the land, with its boundaries, for the people to walk into. The promised land.

If we know anything about the Bible – God's Holy Word – we know that the Israelites stuff it up again. I think the whole theme of the Bible is watching the monumental errors man makes and the subsequent love, grace and mercy our Heavenly Father continues to bestow upon mankind.

So back to freedom, do you think the Reubenites and Gadites would have felt freedom in their new land? For a time, maybe, but soon a dissatisfaction would have settled in their hearts – they would want more. We always want more. If freedom is not, as the dictionary describes, "the power or right to act, speak or think as one wants, or the state of not being imprisoned or enslaved", then what is it?

I believe that the only way to be truly free - be it in confinement, rich, poor, single, married, alone, surrounded by those we love or whatever our circumstances – is Christ!

Galatians 3:23-29 (ESV) *²³ Now before faith came, we were held captive under the law, imprisoned until the coming faith would be revealed. ²⁴So then, the law was our guardian until Christ came, in order that we might be justified by faith. ²⁵But now that faith has* *come, we are no longer under a guardian, ^{26}for in Christ Jesus you are all sons of God, through faith. ^{27}For as many of you as were baptized into Christ have put on Christ. ^{28}There is neither Jew nor Greek, there is neither slave nor free, there is no male and female, for you are all one in Christ Jesus. ^{29}And if you are Christ's, then you are Abraham's offspring, heirs according to promise.*

What does that mean though? I think that freedom is a state of being, not an actionable thing. Likewise, with love, you choose to love, even when you wish you could walk away from those who are causing you so much pain and grief. If we gave into our feelings all the time, just imagine – well, simply look at our world today to see the consequences of such behaviour. If it feels good, do it. What a mess! Our modern world, with all the technology and 'freedom', is so bound to 'self' that there is no way mankind is really free.

In conclusion, our 3:16 verse describes a sense of freedom, but true freedom comes from the love of Christ. Acknowledging what He did for us, by His sacrifice on the cross and His resurrection.

Galatians 5:13-14 (ESV) *^{13}For you were called to freedom, brothers. Only do not use your freedom as an opportunity for the flesh, but through love serve one another. ^{14}For the whole law is fulfilled in one word: "You shall love your neighbour as yourself."*

Above all though, I think John 8:34-36 (MSG) sums it up perfectly. *$^{34-36}$Jesus said, "I tell you most solemnly that anyone who chooses a life of sin is trapped in a dead-end life and is, in fact, a slave. A slave is a transient, who can't come and go at will. The Son, though, has an established position, the run of the house. So, if the Son sets you free, you are free through and through.*

Joshua 3:16
(AMP)

16the waters which were flowing down from above stopped and rose up in one mass a great distance away at Adam, the city that is beside Zarethan. Those [waters] flowing downward toward the sea of the Arabah, the Salt Sea, were completely cut off. So the people crossed [the river] opposite Jericho.

My gorgeous first grandson has just turned two. I must tell you, I was so excited about his upcoming birthday, that I think I took on the excitement for him, as he had no idea what was coming. I was counting down the weeks until his special day. I was in awe that it had been two years since he came into the world and, at the same time, *freaking out* that it had already been two years since he came into the world. I couldn't wait until his special day.

I was not disappointed either, he had the best day sharing it with the people who love him. Just quietly, so did I.

I'm now waiting for my upcoming holiday a bit later in the year. This causes me great excitement as I adore the place we are going, but anxiety because I need to fly to get there and well, and that freaks me out.

Waiting! It brings with it good and bad. When it is something we want and look forward to, the waiting can be torturous – but in a good way.

What about when we are waiting to be out of a bad situation?

When I was a young woman, well barely a woman, I was still a child, I met a man who would systematically ruin my life. He made my life a living hell. Without getting into ugly details, the only amazing thing to come out of that mess were my children. I firmly believe God let me endure that hardship for them. He wanted them here and it took that horrid man's DNA to make it happen. For that, I have no regrets.

I cried out in pain nearly every day, begging to be able to get out of this horrendous situation. But fear of what he would do and who he would hurt kept me a prisoner.

My whole marriage, (yes, I married him. It's amazing what fear will make you do) I was looking for an out – in my own strength! Consequently, I endured year after repulsive year.

I suppose it shouldn't be hard to believe, but I had a breakdown. The doctor wanted to admit me to a psychiatric ward for time to heal, but in his heart, he knew I would be trading one prison for another. So, with his help, we were able to convince my husband that I needed to go and stay at my parents' home.

It was in this time that God revealed that He was the only Way out. He was the only way to break free of my prison and He was the only one who had the power to do so.

I spent a couple of weeks with my wonderful parents being nurtured back to a place of health. There was so much prayer in that fortnight that I think my home-town must have been a-buzz with angels.

I was restored, I was resolved, and I was determined to break free. This time though, I knew I was no longer in the driving seat – my precious Father God was.

I'd love to say it was a piece of cake and I went home, packed up and never had another ounce of problems, but alas that was not the case. I did get out, though. I am free, and I am now married to a man who adores me, loves the Lord with all his heart and treats me the way the Father intended a husband to treat his wife.

How does all this relate to the verse today?

The key things I have gleaned from this verse are:

We need to be prepared to pick up where others left off. My parents had been praying solid for me to either get out of that marriage or for God to change that man's heart. The Israelites had waited over 500 years to get out of their prison. They were the generation who would finally cross over the Jordan to the promised land.

We need to accept that we *have* to wait for the good things that have been promised. God's timing is perfect. It is never early, it is never late – it is always, always when it is needed to be. We just don't tend to like the waiting part. Even when the waiting seems eternal, we must, above all, believe that when God says it is going to happen it happens – thus our need for faith.

Imagine the trepidation of the Israelites knowing that tomorrow they were going to cross the river. They must have had doubts, fears and anxiety – was it really going to happen? Were they going to stuff it up again and not get to cross? Was God really going to go before them?

Don't we all have these feelings about things we want to change or happen? Even when the promise is happening, or going to happen, there will be obstacles. For the Israelites, there was a great big river they needed to get over!

For me, I guess I had my own river to cross.

When these obstacles occur, we must step out, step up, be accountable, even when to our own eyes, it seems futile.

The people had to follow the Ark, they had to trust that the priests would do as commanded (step into the Jordon]) and they had to trust that God would create a path.

None of the events would have taken place to get the people across the river if they had not taken that first step!

They had to prepare their hearts before the Lord, they had to trust He would do as He said He would, and they had to make the first move to show their trust and faith that the King of Kings, Lord of Lords would carry them forward.

And above all, trust God!

For it is only when it is beyond our own ability to fix the situation that God is free to do His thing.

When we accept, and take our hands off the situation – God lifts us up and carries us to our destination. That the situation will never change if we do not surrender – in surrender we are free.

We must take that first step of faith. This is why they call it a leap of faith.

We are our own worst prison guard. We bind ourselves to the things of earth and wish it were different. We make decisions and forget, like a stone tossed in the water, there will be outflowing ripples. As humans, we forget that we are tiny specks in the big picture. Just think of what happens to you on a windy day – you are blown from pillar to post.

Rebellion, stubbornness and impatience have always been my weakest characteristics. I have, over the years, tempered the rebellion, but stubbornness and impatience still plague me. It is so stupid, for it is when I admit *I can't do this* that God does His part! Yet my human nature persists on being right, in control and steadfast in what I think is so.

My prayer is that God releases this in me, and in you. The kicker here, is that I, again, must be prepared to let it go so God can do what He does. I pray to be able continually walk forward and know that my God, my Saviour is clearing a path for me. The obstacles are no longer there, and I do not need to worry.

Ephesians 3:12 (NLV) *Because of Christ and our faith in him, we can now come boldly and confidently into God's presence.*

2 Corinthians 3:12 (NLT) *Since this new way gives us such confidence, we can be very bold.*

He is in control; He sets us free. Walk boldly forward knowing that God has cleared the way. He has sent others before you to step out on your behalf. You will cross *your* Jordan on dry ground, into the promised land He has prepared for you!

Judges 3:16
(NLT)

16So Ehud made a double-edged dagger that was about a foot long, and he strapped it to his right thigh, keeping it hidden under his clothing.

What possible relevance can this scripture have to us? We will endeavour to put this together, but the one thing I know. as Paul says in 2 Timothy 3:16-17 (NLT)

16All Scripture is inspired by God and is useful to teach us what is true and to make us realize what is wrong in our lives. It corrects us when we are wrong and teaches us to do what is right., 17God uses it to prepare and equip his people to do every good work.

So, with that in mind, let us explore what this verse means together.

I guess we need to put this verse into context of what was happening at that time. The Israelites were at it again, doing the wrong thing. They had forgotten their God and chosen the sins of the flesh. Instead of worshipping God their Creator, they chose to bow down to the Baals & Asherahs, those of the Canaanites. They had become so bogged down in their lifestyle choices that they didn't see their worlds crashing around them.

Then in typical Israelite fashion, the proverbial hit the fan and they cried out to God. Because God loved them and had made a covenant with them He rescued them. Once their feet were set on the right path again they lived holy lives, right? No. They. Didn't. They went back to their sinful way. The whole chapter is talking about the crying out, the rescuing, the return to sinning.

What the?????

Think about this for a moment. When you are hurting, and you need to be rescued – do you cry out for help? When you have been brought out of the danger by your rescuer, do you then spend the rest of your life serving that person?

Now, wait a minute you say, they were rescued by God! How could they not?!

The problem is they had become so caught up in their sin, they forgot to see God as Creator, Almighty, the One True God. They just saw Him as a way out of their mess.

Maybe they had become so caught up in their lifestyle choices that when bad stuff happened to them, they thought it was par for the course. When they were rescued, maybe they just thought, *phew, our luck has changed.*

It is only when we see who has saved us, for who He really is, and repent of our ways, do we have a chance to be truly set free.

I became a born again Christian when I was twelve years old. I went forward in front of two thousand people and declared my love for my Lord Jesus.

Approximately a year later, my grandmother died before my eyes. I was gutted, devastated and completely lost as to how a loving God could let my grandmother die. This was the start of my journey to self-destruction.

Now, if anyone asked, of course I was a Christian, but I did not live the life, really. I chose my own path. I got into messes and cried out to God to fix it. He did. I went on my merry way and got myself into mischief again.

What the????

Why would I do that? Could I not see the King of Kings, Lord of Lords, stepping in and rescuing me?

I spent most of my young-adult life bouncing between euphoric love for Jesus to, *meh* love for Him.

I then came to a place where my life was truly a mess and I called out to God, yet somehow this time, I knew I needed to completely repent. I had to let go of my life and allow God to shift me. I physically moved as well - my children and I relocated to a city on a mountain. I often joked that God wanted me to get closer to Him, so He moved me to a mountain.

Since that time, I have never wavered in my love for Jesus. I stand firm and each day I feel it gets stronger, I am bolder for the Lord and I will never go back to the valley.

I believe that when I was twelve, I made the choice in a hyped-up arena and it didn't permeate through to my inner being. I met Jesus, as you meet someone at a party. I didn't get to know Him. I left the party and even though I kept the memory of the encounter, I didn't let it reach the inner part of me. So, in my opinion, because I didn't have this deep-seated encounter with Him; I could let Him go all too easy. He became my genie in a bottle who I would call upon when I was in a sticky situation and then I had the nerve to blame Him for not keeping me out of the mess that I created!

When I had an encounter with Him – and moved to my mountain – it was different. I took accountability for my actions, I repented of who I had become, and I allowed myself to become so completely submerged in Him that I could never let Him go. He changed me from the inside out. But I allowed it to happen for I truly loved Him and wanted to please Him. So, I opened my heart and let the changes happen.

I am still a sinner, I still make colossal mistakes. Yet, this time, I turn to God to get back on the path . I don't spurn in anger at *'how can my life be so bad, blah, blah, blah...'*

Now, back to Ehud. Ehud lived in a dangerous time, so carrying a concealed dagger was not unheard of. He was a left-handed man, and therefore was considered, in some ways, disabled. There was nothing special about him in any way. He was not the chosen one to save them all. He was in the right place at the right time and, in essence, was an errand boy.

Ehud was only heading off to the King Eglon of Moab to pay a tribute to keep him happy with his people. I am not sure he even intended to kill the king at the time. Yet again, the Israelites had cried out to the Lord their God and He, who had made a covenant with them, rescued them, using a simple man, such as Ehud. By his killing the king, it allowed the Israelites to form an army and wipe out the Moabs. They had peace for 80 years.

This might seem that they had finally got it right, but sadly, again no, they were just tired of being imprisoned and cried out. Truth is, they still had not fully repented.

They had not had their mountain experience. They were still in the valley, living with those who did not love the Lord God. Maybe they thought they could change the Canaanites - to teach them to love God - yet it was the Canaanites who changed the Israelites.

Why?

I think it is because when we let go of our anchor (God) we are just empty vessels bobbing in the sea at the mercy of the waves and winds. We will be easily led from one harbour to the next. It is only through our anchor, Jesus, that we can hold fast to the truth and not be at the mercy of what the world can throw at us.

The things I have gleaned from this verse are:

We think we can change people, but they change us if we are not securely anchored to God.

Idolatry and disbelief will take hold of us quicker than we can blink and it will erode our very being before we can even realise that we have let go of our anchor.

God is our deliverer and He will always rescue us when we call. He just wants us to do it with a repentant heart.

Flawed people rise-up for God. We are all flawed, so this is good news for all of us. All it takes is a heart for God and He can use us mightily.

Sin cannot go unpunished. As much as God loves us, He cannot abide by sin. Our poor choices need to be punished. Our continued cycle of sin / rescue will never change until we repent. We will still need to take our medicine, yet somehow when given by our loving Father, it is bearable, and we are that much more eager to please in the future.

Jesus took our eternal punishment. When we turn to Him, we will never again have to fear death (which is the punishment for sin) for He has set us free.

And above all, the most important thing I have learned from this verse is that people may forget, but God never forgets His covenant.

He chose to love us, He chose to save us, and He will never, ever go back on His Word.

Ruth 3:16
(NLT)

16When Ruth went back to her mother-in-law, Naomi asked, "What happened, my daughter?" Ruth told Naomi everything Boaz had done for her,

I have read Ruth several times over the years and never put much into the story, I am sad to confess. Ruth was the daughter-in-law of Naomi. Super briefly I will give the outline.

Naomi lived in Canaan and there was a major famine so Naomi's hubby, Elimelech, moved her and their two boys to Moab. After they moved, Elimelech died. This meant that the torch was passed to the sons to provide for Naomi. The boys married Moabite women. One of these was Ruth. We move on about 10 years and the sons also die. Naomi is a seriously ticked off woman.

She decides she had better head back to Judah, where she had been told God would provide for her. Her two, now widowed daughters-in-law, went to go with her.

Before too long, Naomi tells the girls, "Look, I am an old broad, I can't have any more kids and even if I did, it's not like they will be much use to you. Go back to your land and find another hubby to provide for you. I'm having a major pity-party-for-one and God doesn't love me anymore, so I am useless to you." Paraphrase of Ruth 1:8-13

Now, at first, I thought that Naomi's concern for her daughters-in-law was for them. I think as we read on we note that it is actually out of selfishness that she doesn't want them around. After all, more mouths to feed on no income.

Ruth shocks us all with her response, *[16] "Do not urge me to leave you or to turn back from following you; for where you go, I will go, and where you lodge, I will lodge. Your people will be my people, and your God, my God. [17] Where you die, I will die, and there I will be buried. May the Lord do the same to me [as He has done to you], and more also, if anything but death separates me from you."* Ruth 1:16-17

Wow! You will soon see that this is just the start of an insight of the character of Ruth.

Anyway, let's move on. Naomi and Ruth head back to Bethlehem and Naomi kicks up her pity-party into a higher gear and bemoans, to all who will lend an ear, how ticked she is with God. She even changed her name to Mara (bitter). See Ruth 1:20 (AMP)

She's so cranky, she seems to forget that she returned to Bethlehem for she believed that God would provide. She is so caught up in her bitterness and anger towards God that she bypasses His plan and sets out to orchestrate a way that Ruth can provide for them instead.

She sends Ruth to work for their relative Boaz. Boaz has some serious coin and Naomi starts to scheme ways that she can marry off Ruth, which, in turn, means that she will be provided for. Naomi has two things in her favour, in her thinking. Firstly, Ruth has already made a vow to Naomi to always be with her and secondly, Boaz is a relative, which means he is duty bound to provide for them.

So, let's move to our verse of the day. Seems innocent enough, doesn't it? The truth is though, Naomi tried to manipulate Boaz by sending Ruth to him late at night to try and seduce him while his judgement was impaired by wine – you'll have to read Ruth 3 to get the whole picture.

Boaz turns out to be a man of integrity and Ruth, who came from a non-religious background, shows more character and love for God than Naomi does. Without compromising either himself or Ruth, Boaz says he will make an honest woman out of Ruth and he will continue to provide for Naomi, too. All ends well. It could have been very different, though. I think it was only through Boaz and Ruth's honourable behaviour that God blessed them.

What I glean from this verse is that we can all be 'Naomis' and get caught up in doing our own thing and not waiting upon the Lord for help.

We can all let bitterness and anger take control, and lose sight of the big picture and start to take on the role of god in our lives.

We can get very good at pretending we are doing God's work when we are really only trying to feather our own nests – that's a pretty tough pill to swallow when it is written down, hey!

But let us flip over to Ruth's example of what this passage means :

Obedience.

We can choose obedience – to God and to others. When we choose to honour our elders, we are in turn honouring God.

Reflecting God's love in our actions.

By following Naomi's commands, Ruth was reflecting God's love by doing as she was told – yet she also managed to honour herself, Boaz and God by choosing her words carefully and trusting that Boaz was the man she believed him to be.

Putting other's needs before our own desires.

I think Ruth understood what Naomi was up to, but knew it was important to Naomi, so she did as she was told. Sadly, Naomi wasn't quite so caring of Ruth's reputation – she was putting her own desires before anything else.

God always provides a way.

Ruth was a woman of great character and God blessed her in that by ensuring that she was taken care of and not compromised in her actions.

God loves the lowly and downtrodden.

Ruth was not an Israelite, she was a Moabite – therefore she wasn't in the 'chosen', yet God picked her up, dusted her off and through her, her descendant David was born – AKA Jesus' family tree. That's a big deal! God can take any situation and turn it to His Glory.

Doing the 'best' we can with what we have.

Ruth knew she had to obey Naomi – she was, after all, living under her roof and, as the junior, she had to help provide for Naomi. Naomi sending Ruth out in the middle of the night was potentially a pretty bad thing for Ruth – she could have been seen and she would have been branded a harlot and she also ran the risk of tarnishing Boaz's name – for there was a relative closer to Naomi than that of Boaz. The rules back then were strict!

Doing right in God's eyes as opposed to what we see as right in our own.

Naomi did what was right in her eyes. Ruth tried to do what was right in God's.

We always have a choice – do we choose flesh or spirit?

When we choose flesh, we separate ourselves from God. Choosing God, even when it seems impossible means we allow the God of the Impossible to move mightily in our lives.

Being bold enough to ask God for what we need.

We need to come boldly to God and ask for what we need.

"Therefore, let us confidently approach the throne of grace to receive mercy and find grace whenever we need help." Hebrews 4:16 (NET)

Honouring others enough, but ensuring all honour goes to God.

Always honour those who are in our circle, but remember they are human, they are fallible, just as we are. So, ensure that the highest honour always goes to God. Seek his Word in all things.

"If you remain in me and my words remain in you, ask whatever you want, and it will be done for you." John 15:7 (NET)

Choose our counsel wisely – those who appear godly may not be. Look at the whole picture of the person.

Ruth followed Naomi, as Naomi was her mother-in-law. She chose to learn the ways of her God. Yet, if she hadn't had a real encounter with God, she would have become just as bitter towards God as Naomi was.

Ruth obeyed Naomi, but I feel she took her wise counsel from Boaz as he was a truer example of God's love than Naomi.

Always look at the person's whole life and their actions before taking on what they say. Every person who walks the earth is imperfect, yet some take these imperfections and lay them at the foot of the cross – thus the decisions and choices they make in life are directed by God. Others take their imperfections and try, within their own strength, to get it all together.

Anything worth having is worth working for.

Anything that comes too easy, is too easily lost. It seems to be the way of it. It is when we have had to sacrifice for something that we tend to hold onto it more securely.

God sacrificed His Son for us! He gave us the whole world in Jesus. He did all the hard work. Maybe that is why Christians struggle; we think we must work for God's Love, Grace and Mercy. We don't think it is something we should just receive without working for it.

The gift of God's love is easy, keeping a hold of it and abiding in it is not as easy. We must work at our relationships – be those here on earth or the one with the King of Kings.

When we love here on earth, we make allowances, we make sacrifices, we change for those we love. We ask them, 'What can I do to show you I love you?'

When we love God, when we come before the foot of the cross of Jesus, we can lay our burdens down. He will lift us up and restore us. His love is so powerful, that we in turn learn how to love like Jesus.

So as much as we can't earn God's love, we can work towards loving Him in a way that honours Him above all else.

May we walk in God's love boldly and know that He goes before us in all things. He has provided a way for us and all we need to do in return is love Him and love others.

³⁷Jesus replied, "'You must love the LORD your God with all your heart, all your soul, and all your mind.' ³⁸This is the first and greatest commandment. ³⁹A second is equally important: 'Love your neighbour as yourself.' ⁴⁰The entire law and all the demands of the prophets are based on these two commandments." Matthew 22:37-40 (NLT)

1 Samuel 3:16
(NLT)

16But Eli called out to him, "Samuel, my son."

"~~Here~~ I am," Samuel replied.

I remember this story well from my childhood Sunday School days – but I have to confess – I think we were only taught up to the verses where Eli told Samuel it is the Lord who calls you, not me.

⁸So the Lord called Samuel a third time. And he stood and went to Eli and said, "Here I am, for you did call me." Then Eli understood that it was the Lord [who was] calling the boy. ⁹So Eli said to Samuel, "Go, lie down, and it shall be that if He calls you, you shall say, 'Speak, Lord, for Your servant is listening.'" So Samuel went and lay down in his place. 1 Samuel 3:8-9 (AMP)

Here I am, many years later, reading this for the 3:16 devotionals and I see this passage in a whole new light.

Imagine being Samuel. At the time of hearing God call to him,

Samuel did not yet know the Lord (1 Sam 3:7). So of course, when he heard a voice calling, he assumed it was Eli.

We also need to remember that this was set in a time when *"The word of the Lord was rare and precious in those days; visions [that is, new revelations of divine truth] were not widespread."* 1 Samuel 3:1.

God wasn't talking, because man wasn't listening!

Samuel, at the time of his encounter with the Living God, was probably in his mid-teens. Still a boy, not yet a man. God, however, felt that he was ready to hear His Word and that he was also ready to act upon what he would hear.

If you are like me, you remember the part about God speaking to Samuel, not what He actually said. If you are like me, you don't recall being taught it, or maybe you have just blocked it out - it ain't pretty.

Before we get to that though, let's take a moment to think about Samuel. A boy who did not yet know the Lord. From the sounds of the way Eli was doing things, if it were left up to him, Samuel would never know the Lord, just as Eli's own sons did not know the Lord.

The key word here is 'yet'. Samuel did not *yet* know the Lord – meaning, upon his encounter, he KNEW the Lord, toot-sweet!

Eli's sons never knew the Lord. How incredibly sad, considering their father was a Jewish priest who was supposed to be serving God at the tabernacle. Eli's sons never knew the Lord, for Eli's example clearly did not demonstrate an undeniably God-filled life. He was a prime example of why God had stopped talking.

Now Samuel was a teen who had been living in the tabernacle as Eli's 'protégé', which I think may have just meant errand boy, for Eli was old. He wasn't really getting an education on who the Lord God was (I am assuming this, for if he was, he would have known God). Anyway, the point is, Samuel hears a voice, he not-surprisingly assumes it is Eli, and he is used to doing things for Eli so up he gets up and expects to do whatever it is that Eli requires. Three times he hears the call and three times he assumes it has to be Eli.

Eli, upon the third visit from Samuel, has a penny drop moment and realises, *oh, whoops it's God!*

Now, the interesting part – both Eli and Samuel have a choice to make. Eli had to choose to tell Samuel that it is God, when He calls again, answer Him, not me. Fair enough, pretty easy to share that tidbit of info with the boy. Although, I wonder, just how easy it was to tell Samuel that it was God. It seems to me that the priests of the time were so far from communing with God, that it must have been a bit hard to grasp that God is speaking at all, forget to a boy and not a priest. But Eli gets his *aha* moment and shares with Samuel.

Let's pause a moment to take in the gravity of what happens to Samuel, just a boy who did not yet know the Lord. Set in a time when no one really heard from God. Now, supposedly, the one true God is trying to have a chat.

The Choice!

The defining moment of Samuel's life.

He chose to believe it was the Lord God speaking to him and

he answered.

¹⁰ Then the Lord came and stood and called as at the previous times, "Samuel! Samuel!" Then Samuel answered, "Speak, for Your servant is listening."

This is the moment when the boy Samuel became a man of God. He had a choice and chose the Word of the Lord, not the ways of the priests. He chose obedience over fear and confusion. He chose to believe and act upon the words his teacher had told him. He chose to prepare his heart before the Lord.

The real kicker here is that what God chose to reveal to this boy was huge.

¹¹The Lord said to Samuel, "Behold, I am about to do a thing in Israel at which both ears of everyone who hears it will ring. ¹²On that day I will carry out against Eli everything that I have spoken concerning his house (family), from beginning to end. ¹³Now I have told him that I am about to judge his house forever for the sinful behaviour which he knew [was happening], because his sons were bringing a curse on themselves [dishonouring and blaspheming God] and he did not rebuke them. ¹⁴Therefore I have sworn to the house of Eli that the sinful behaviour of Eli's house (family) shall not be atoned for by sacrifice or offering forever."
1 Samuel 11-14

Like, are you serious? Imagine hearing that!

Interestingly, God had already tried to tell Eli this was happening, so did Eli not hear, or did he choose to ignore God's warning?

So, we finally get to our verse, *¹⁶But Eli called out to him, "Samuel, my son." "Here I am," Samuel replied.*

Again, another choice, tell Eli what he had heard from God, or ignore it, or maybe even make it sound less horrifying than it was.

In verse 15 it states ...*But Samuel was afraid to tell the vision to Eli.*

I think when we try to do things in our own strength, we fail, pure and simple. When we trust that God has gone before us, the fear may still be there, but we 'feel the fear and do it anyway', Knowing that the great I AM will go before us.

Now, maybe for Samuel, it was the warning that Eli spat at him that convinced him to share. I wonder if Eli knew what he was asking Samuel to reveal he might not have pulled that particular card out of the deck?!

¹⁶But Eli called Samuel and said, "Samuel, my son." And he answered, "Here I am." ¹⁷Then Eli said, "What is it that He said to you? Please do not hide it from me. May God do the same to you, and more also, if you hide from me anything of all that He said to you." ¹⁸So Samuel told him everything, hiding nothing from him. And Eli said, "It is the Lord; may He do what seems good to Him."

Now I don't know about you, but if someone, who had just heard from God – especially in audible words, that I knew were real – told me something like that, I would have been begging for forgiveness. I would have been pleading my case for my family. Maybe I was too far gone, but my children, let's save them, hey?

It seems, though, that Eli was so far from a real relationship with the living God, that he accepted it as a done deal and in that moment he chose to continue his life of sin.

Let's step back to Samuel. I know he was afraid, the Word of

God says he was, and rightly so. That's a huge thing to tell someone. Maybe Eli's threat did go towards convincing him to share. But I truly believe that God knew that Samuel would reveal His Word to Eli.

God understood that Samuel would be afraid, maybe that's why He allowed Eli to threaten Samuel as a nudge in the right direction. God had big plans for Samuel, and all these came to pass because a young boy – who in an instant became a man of God - chose to listen. He chose to act and chose the ways of the Lord over his own life choices.

We may never be called to prophecy in such a way as Samuel, but every day we are given the opportunity to serve God with our words, our deeds and our emotions.

We can hear that still, small voice and ignore it and carry on in our sinful ways.

Or we, like Samuel, we can say, *"Speak, for Your servant is listening."* 1 Samuel 3:10

The choice is yours.

2 Samuel 3:16
(AMP)

16But her husband went with her, weeping continually behind her as far as Bahurim. Then Abner told him, "Go, return." And he did so.

Okay, this verse has me stumped. I've attempted to sit down and do a devotional on this one for well over a week. I'm finding every excuse under the sun to avoid tackling this. I have no idea what the significance of this verse could be to the big picture of God's love for each of us. This is day ten of sitting in front of my screen and trying to allow God to guide my fingers. What does He want me to say?

Okay, here we go…

I love David. He was a colossal stuff-up. He seemed to start out so awesome – you know, the whole killing Goliath thing. Our childhood is filled with awe of how the little guy can stand up against giants when God is with them. Yes, in the eyes of man he was a first-rate hero. We use the David and Goliath example in many areas of our life – both in the Christian and secular worlds.

I'm still learning the intricacies of David, yet it seemed he went from bad to worse and back to awesome on a daily basis.

Here we are 2 Samuel Chapter 3 and the book opens by outlining all the wives and sons that David had. Ummm... He knew this was a big no-no in God's eyes. One wife, that was the rule of God, yet the rules of the land were, if you are king, have as many as you need or want. Makes you look more powerful.

David, like all of us, seemed to forget at times that he was only where he was, had what he had and oversaw what he did, because God the Creator put him there, for His purpose.

Even though at this stage, the Bible only outlines that David had multiple wives and sons, as we read on, in 1 Chronicles chapter 3 – David's sons show their real colours, cause havoc and reap what they sow. Not a topic for today, just saying.

As we know, David was meant to be king, according to God's purpose, but David's journey to the throne was far from peaceful, safe or simple.

After Saul dies, late 1 Samuel chapter 31, David was supposed to be next king, but Ishbosheth takes power. So, we end up with a civil war situation.

It appears that one of the techniques David used to try and gain back his rightful place on the throne was to get Abner - this is the Abner who had defected to David's side after being accused of stealing Saul's concubine - to bring back Michal, David's wife (yes, another one). Michal was taken from David, by Saul, after David had earned the right to marry her. Long story, politics and all that guff.

We don't know if David truly loved her or just needed her as she was the daughter of Saul, which in turn made David's claim to the throne more real as he was the son-in-law of Saul. Regardless, it seems she was just used as part of a strategy for David to get the throne back.

We are left to assume that Michal was happy with the new 'hubby' arrangement – that is, with Palti. Michal was given to Palti after Saul took her from David.

Which brings me to the verse that I have struggled with. What is the significance of this verse, what does it matter?

Is this verse about David?

Or Palti or Michal?

Or is it about Abner?

David – the war was long and arduous, and it was a struggle for David to remain faithful to God's plan. He needed an edge and taking back his bride seemed to be a good place to start. It also tested Abner's loyalty. Abner had to go and take Michal from Ishbosheth, who was, at the time, the king.

Palti - unfortunately he was a dude who was given a gift that really belonged to someone else – so he was ultimately going to lose. I've tried to investigate the significance of his weeping. There are a couple of theories. One: he truly loved Michal and was going to miss her. Sadly, though, he had no claim as she was still really David's wife. Two: there are reports that they never consummated the relationship and his weeping was a sign of his own pride and wanting to be recognised for not defiling the rightful king's wife.

So, was it about Michal? She was just a pawn in the game of life. Reports state she had loved David, but there is nothing to say he loved her in return. When Saul took her back and gave her to Palti, David all but forgot about her until it seemed to be an opportune time to reclaim his prize.

That brings us to Abner – super-ticked-off-wanting-revenge-against-Ishbosheth-and-supposedly-now-loyal-to-David Abner.

Hmmm. I wonder if it is about all of them! Or is it about you and me?

Can you see a little bit of you in David? Breaking rules to suit yourself? Going ahead of God, thinking that you will 'take care of this one'? Getting caught up in the ways of the world instead of listening to the Creator and the plan He has for your life?

How about Palti?

Have you ever done something you knew you shouldn't and tried to enjoy the 'spoils' of something you haven't earned? Have you tried to get others to recognise that you have done the right thing? (Maybe you have, maybe you haven't, but you feel you have). Have you caused a scene, only to be rebuked and shamed into silence?

Maybe you feel more like Michal?

Powerless to make any choice for yourself, as someone else always seems to be pulling the strings? Love someone who doesn't seem to love you in return? Float along in life, doing what others tell you to do?

Or maybe you are Abner?

Loyal – until you are not? Allow anger to cause you to make rash decisions? Rebuke others, when really you don't have the right to do so? Make promises you can't keep? Hurt anyone in your path to get what you want? Maybe you have also tried to convince people you are doing 'this' for God, when really it is for your own pride?

I hang my head, for I know that I am all of these people and more. I can, sadly, think of times when each of these characteristics have been my own.

This is where I am thankful for how much God loved David. David was a mess – but "*God called him a man after my own heart*" Acts 13:22. What!!!! That just fills me with so much joy and happiness, I cannot tell you.

If David, who throughout the Bible stuffed-up over and over, is a man after God's heart, then there is hope for me and for you.

The thing that makes him so special is that he recognised his shortcomings and took them to God over and over. He never tired of saying, "God I am such a fool, I am so unworthy, I am such a dunce head – but You love me so much, that none of that matters. Use me Lord God for all You are worth, and I will be Your humble servant until the day You take me home to be with You." (Read Psalms – you'll get the drift about David)

David in all his failings as a human, gives us hope – we can be David, Palti, Michal or Abner over and over in life, that's ok – the answer is we take our mistakes, or pride our anger our rebellion, our sense of powerlessness and so on, to the foot of the cross and we lay it there. Then we get up, dust ourselves off and take the hand of Jesus and keep walking into the life He has planned for us.

1 Kings 3:16
(NLT)

16 "Some time later two prostitutes came to the king to have an argument settled."

When I first read what the 1 Kings 3:16 verse was, I laughed. "Oh boy, I thought 2 Samuel 3:16 was a challenge – what do I do here? God, you are certainly taking me out of my comfort zone!"

As with each of these verses, I read the whole chapter, try and get an understanding of when it was set and what is really being said here. Then of course, I write the interpretation that I feel God is giving me to share.

I want to go a bit further back in the chapter to Solomon's prayer. When I read it, I got goose-bumps and I cried. Let me share.

1 Kings 6-9 (NLT) *⁶ Then Solomon said, "You have shown Your servant David my father great lovingkindness, because he walked before You in faithfulness and righteousness and with uprightness of heart toward You; and You have kept for him this great loving-*

kindness, in that You have given him a son to sit on his throne, as it is today. ⁷ So now, O Lord my God, You have made Your servant king in place of David my father; and as for me, I am but a little boy [[d]in wisdom and experience]; I do not know how to go out or come in [that is, how to conduct business as a king]. ⁸ Your servant is among Your people whom You have chosen, a great people who are too many to be numbered or counted. ⁹ So give Your servant an understanding mind and a hearing heart [with which] to judge Your people, so that I may discern between good and evil. For who is able to judge and rule this great people of Yours?"

Wow! Imagine asking God for that!

Imagine you have the world at your feet – pretty well everything is yours – you are after all the king. Instead of asking for money, wealth, fame, a long life of luxury, Solomon asks for wisdom and a loving heart towards God's people. Solomon didn't even call them his people – as a king he could have – but instead he gave all glory to God.

I cried for I know how far short I come to this kind of thinking. My prayer life sucks, really, in the big scheme of things. All too often my prayer is for my own comfort and the comfort of those I love.

Now God, Who Was, Who Is and Who Always will be, turns around and says, yep of course, and not only that, because you weren't asking for all the trimmings of being a king, well you can have that too. See 1 Kings 10-14.

Now, we move onto our verse, *¹⁶"Some time later two prostitutes came to the king to have an argument settled."*

We are led to believe that Solomon hasn't really done anything significant with this wisdom, for the chapter ends with all the people of Israel in awe about what Solomon said and did regarding the two prostitutes.

So, Solomon is in a situation here where the 'rubber meets the road', so to speak. He is confronted with two harlots – so, in essence, women of little value in that time.

He could have just told them to go away, stop wasting my time. You are not even worthy to stand in my presence.

He could have let one of his officers of the court deal with their argument.

He could have had them both put to death for arguing with him – in his own palace.

What did he do though?

Okay, so overview of what happened – two prostitutes shared a house, within days of each other they gave birth to a child each. One of the women, during the night, rolled on top of her baby and killed it. She did a bit of a sneaky, sneaky and took her dead baby into the other woman's room and did the ol' switcheroo – thinking that the rightful mum wouldn't recognise the switch. So, both mum's wake the next morning. One has a dead baby, one has a live one. The mum of the dead baby knows that the baby in her arms is not hers – the other one is. So, an argument ensues and next thing you know they are before the king presenting their case. Each arguing that the live baby is theirs. See 1 Kings 16-22.

It appears that Solomon didn't even hesitate – he called for his sword. He told the women, 'Let's just cut the baby in half and you can have half each!' V24

The interesting part is that there are two completely different responses from the women. One says, you beauty, lets have at it. The classic 'if I can't have him neither can you' attitude.

The other, is deeply moved by the king and says, no, let her have this child – do not kill him.

Solomon, in his wisdom, tested the women, tested their love for the child, tested their hearts. He knew the rightful mother would never harm her child. So, of course, he awarded the living child to the mother who was prepared to lose her son, so he could live.

Her love was so great for her child, she was prepared to put his needs before her own wants. She loved him so much that she was prepared to let him go – to be with someone, who was obviously just greedy – so he could live.

She didn't think about her own heart, her own pain. When it came down to it – it was all about the future wellbeing of her son that counted.

How often though in life are we the woman who says – have at it – cut the baby? Maybe not so dramatic, but how often have we put our own desires before what is right, or the needs of others?

I asked a question the other day, and I am still not sure I have an answer.

I believe God has a plan and a purpose for each of us, a path we are to walk in His Glory, for His purpose – this I am sure we can all agree.

My question is, 'what happens when your supposed path clashes with someone else's?'

What I mean is, in your mind, and maybe your heart, you see the way something should be, but someone else sees what they want, or feel is right for their life. For each of you to get what you believe is the right path for you, means the other may be hurt.

Think of a husband and wife. Husband gets a transfer to another town, wife wants to stay as her friends and her job are where they currently live. Up to this point, they both feel they have been on the same journey. If they are both following God's path – what is the answer? If they go, the husband's path is being fulfilled, if they stay the wife's is. It seems that one must miss out.

I've struggled with this – but I truly believe that, in my 3:16 journey, I have found the answer.

Love!

True love seeks for others.

Selfish 'love' seeks for self.

Yes, it might hurt the wife to have to move, but God has the bigger picture in hand – He knows what lies in wait for the woman in the new town. He knows that the path she is on currently will only improve if she takes a detour. Yes, it will hurt in the short term – but God's plan is always bigger. Conversely, if they stay the husband would be okay, too. (Don't want to be sexist here).

Our mother in this story was prepared to lose her child to another, who, in her actions of killing her first child through carelessness, is probably not the best role model for her child. Regardless, she was prepared to let him go.

Let her baby go to live a life without her. Yes, her heart would have been breaking, as any mother reading this would know. Yet, somehow, she loved enough to let go. See her love was true, for her love was for others, not for her own self.

We think that when we love, we have to hold on with everything we have, yet in truth, sometimes it means letting go.

Pain goes with the territory of love. I think it is the only way to know there is true love – by how much it hurts.

Both our main characters in this book are living out of love. Solomon lived out of love and reverence for God, to do what He wanted, not out of glory for his own self. The rightful mother, out of love, gave up her child, so he could live, even though she would have been beyond words devastated.

Love!

I think the only way we can truly love, is to know that our God, our Creator, our Saviour has the big picture in hand. We need to let go of what we are holding, so we can reach out and receive what is truly waiting for us all. We live in our insulated worlds, protecting our hearts – at what cost really? When things are tough for me, I say, 'Let go and Let God!'

Loosen the grip you have on the things you hold dear and allow them the opportunity to fly. Because maybe, just maybe, the path you have chosen will lead to destruction – for we cannot see around the bend. But God sees the whole landscape, He sees the bends, the twists, the turns.

Let go of what you are holding, then take the Hand of your Saviour and soar!

2 Kings 3:16
(NLT)

> 16and he said, "This is what the LORD says: This dry valley will be filled with pools of water!

To clarify, the 'he', who spoke what the Lord said is Elisha – the successor of Elijah. A little background on Elisha: he was the trainee under Elijah the great prophet. When it was time for Elijah to depart Earth, he didn't do this in the normal fashion. God took him up to heaven in a whirlwind and a chariot of fire. Pretty darn cool. Elisha wanted more than anything to follow God and be blessed by Him. So, he asked Elijah for a double portion of his gifting. God and Elijah answered him accordingly – but it was only because of Elisha's dogged persistence. You can read the actual events in 2 Kings 2.

On our journey of looking at all of the Holy Bible's Chapter 3 Verse 16's, there are some doozies. What do they mean and, more to the point, how can we take relevance in a verse, that seems so random, into our own lives? I have come to realise that every word in the Bible has a meaning and a reason.

As I read through the Old Testament, I often think that the people of the day treated God's prophets as their excuse for not seeking God themselves. I realise that it was not until Jesus that these people even thought they could consult God directly – they saw Him as terrifying and distant. Jesus closed the gap. What I mean is that they seemed to use the prophets as their genies – *'I have a request, fix it'; 'Oh I am in the poop again, get me out'; 'Darn the enemy are coming, tell us how to get out of this mess'* and so on.

They didn't know, care or realise that God wanted to be a part of their everyday; the little things, the waking up, the going to sleep, the smile for the love of their life, the daily grind, the ruling of the kingdom, the first glance at their new born child they held in their arms. God wanted to share the journey of life then, just as He does now.

Too often, then as in today, God is consulted as an afterthought. *Whoops, my bad, I'm in a pickle!* It's like that show, *I'm A Celebrity, Get Me Out Of Here*. We think because we have a loose standing with God He should fix things. It is like we have reduced Him to a genie where we can rub the lamp and He pops out and fixes things according to our wishes.

In 2 Kings 3 there is 'a trouble' brewing. Wasn't there always in the Old Testament? The kings went off on their own accord and realised that they hadn't thought it through. They get out into the middle of nowhere and then realise, *'Oh man, there's no water, we are right royally in the doodoo'*. Solution – *'Oh yeah, let's call on a prophet, better late than never, hey!'*

They find Elisha, who, I might add, is not all that willing to help them, for up to this point these kings have sought after pagan gods. Elisha is like, *go off and consult them – you aren't really interested in the living God, so why should I help you?!*

Now, interestingly, Jehoram (king of Israel in Samaria) said no, I need your help. he stood his ground and needed God's favour. Elisha, being a true man of God, saw the opportunity for God to be glorified and said I will help only because I have regard for Jehoshaphat (king of Judah).

So, Elisha called upon God and God filled the land with water for the people and the animals. But because He is the one True God, He took it a step further and said, I'll also give you the Moabites (that's who they were going after).

Now it would be lovely to think that after this, these kings all turned from their self-serving ways and sought God in all things – sadly this is not the case. They continue on as they had before, seeking prophets when they needed something fixed.

One's argument could be that in their day they saw God as distant – but let's think of earlier in the Bible, of our great heroes Moses, Aaron, Abraham and so on. They didn't consult prophets, they sought God. They were still a tad scared of Him, they still saw Him as distant, but they made a relationship with Him.

I guess what I glean from this verse is that God is the God who answers prayers. He goes above and beyond what we ask for. He gives us far more than we could ever dream of even asking.

Ultimately though, He doesn't want to be your genie, He wants to be a part of you. That's why He sent Jesus. He gave us the Holy Spirit to dwell within us – so we don't have to seek prophets or seek fortune tellers or mystics. He doesn't want us to consult Him just when we get in the poop. He wants us to relate with Him in our everyday – this I might add, can prevent the poop happening in the first place.

How do we hear God today? We dwell in His Word. We spend time soaking up His guidance through the Holy Bible. It's a slow methodical journey, it is a day to day walk. We walk this journey with a heart full of knowing we are never alone. We have the Spirit of God within us. We don't need to call for God to send fire down or come to us in our times of need.

He is already here. He is watching, waiting and reaching out to you every second and every minute of every hour of your life.

What do you have to do? Take the outstretched hand of Jesus, invite Him into your heart and let Him dwell within you.

God's promise - you will never walk alone again.

1 Chronicles 3:16
(NLT)

16 The successors of Jehoiakim were his son Jehoiachin and his brother Zedekiah.

Dictionaries refers to a *chronicle* as a chronological and factual account of historical or important events.

This leads us to understand that Chronicles 1 and 2 in the Bible are an account of events that took place. 1 Chronicles 3:16 lists the names of King David's sons and successors. What makes David's line so incredible is that the crown was passed down father to son for seventeen generations.

Jesus comes from David's line. David was chosen by God to be king – he was the runt of the litter, he was not even considered worthy to be called for the line-up *(See 1 Sam 16)*

God does not look at outward appearances though, does He? He looks at the heart, and he found David's older brothers lacking the characteristics He required for His plan to be carried forward.

When I read 1 Chronicles and saw how many children David had to so many different females, I was thinking to myself, *'Okay God, what on Earth do you want me to do with this verse – explain that David was just an overly sexual man who wanted to sow his seeds across the globe?!'*

So, as I have done with all of these verses, when they become too hard. I put them aside and wait until God gives me something.

I am sure the more Bible savvy of you will understand the genealogy and the theology behind all of this, but all I can do is what is placed on my heart.

David's line leads us to Jesus! That's good enough for me.

David's messed up, dysfunctional, occasionally self-willed, defiant, 'go-my-own-way', ragtag line led to Jesus.

Wow!

Think about that for a moment.

David was long gone before Jesus came to Earth, his descendants to Jesus are approximately 41 (by Luke's account. Luke was a highly educated, details man, a physician who wanted to catch as much detail as possible. Matthew's account there are 28, he wasn't always as detailed as Luke) Either way, there are still a lot of people to make all sorts of mistakes between David and Jesus. The family line could have gone haywire anywhere and Jesus, in truth, because of the way humans operate should not have come from that line. BUT! He did! That means God chose it that way. He chose David, He chose you, He chose me!

Think of your own dysfunctional family tree – I'm sure you

have one – just as I do. My tree is so muddled I don't even know the truth beyond my father.

What humbles me and brings me to my knees in thanksgiving and praise to God Almighty, is that my lineage does not matter. Either does yours!

God does not care where you came from or what, in your past, led you to make the decisions you made. He has had you in the palm of His hand since before you were formed in your mother's womb.

Jeremiah 1:5 (NLT) *5"I knew you before I formed you in your mother's womb. Before you were born I set you apart and appointed you as my prophet to the nations."*

You are exactly where you are supposed to be. You are exactly who God knew you would be, and you are precisely who He loves, in spite of your ups and downs, challenges, good and bad, heartbreak and elation.

I look back over my life to some of the pits of despair and, at the time, I wondered how on God's green Earth could any of this be for His Glory?

Currently I am in the midst of one of my greatest highs simultaneously with one of my greatest lows. Embracing the high, means the low is ever closer too. I am torn, conflicted and up and down like a yo-yo.

Truth be told, some days I am simply too immersed in my confliction, I don't cope. I withdraw and spend the day with my Jesus crying, laughing, begging for answers.

Yet, because of the journey I have been on and the closer I come to my God, the more I wait for God to reveal what is the greater purpose in all this.

Can you imagine what it must have been like for the disciples – the waiting! They would have thought it was over, done, finished – just as Jesus declared from the cross – it is finished! John 19:30

Everything they had been through, all the words Jesus had spoken, the miracles He performed, the journey they shared, must have seemed so distant to them in that waiting.

Three days later though, the King of Kings, Lord of Lords rose from the dead as He promised He would, and all that pain vanished in an instant. They knew He was the great I AM.

The great I AM is working in your life, too – He is right there with you in your messed-up genealogy. He is with you through all of your mistakes, smart decisions ups and downs. He will never let you out of His grip. You are His.

And as for me, that is the best place in the world to be - safe in the arms of my Jesus.

(NLT)

16He made a network of interwoven chains and used them to decorate the tops of the pillars. He also made 100 decorative pomegranates and attached them to the chains.

We look at the genealogy of David and wonder how on Earth there is going to be a son, who will have enough character, to become king when David's time comes to pass the reigns.

As with all things, God was in control of the situation and had just the man in mind – Solomon.

We believe Solomon to the be wisest, richest and most influential king of his time. This didn't just happen. He actually prayed that he would be wise, full of knowledge and be able to reign over his people according to what God wanted.

Due to his selfless prayer, God not only granted him wisdom but immeasurable wealth as well. See 2 Chronicles 3:8-13

He took his wealth and created a temple for God. It was seriously lavish, and he spared no coinage to make it happen.

This brings us to our verse. This is just one snippet of the decorations he had built for God's Holy Place. Throughout the chapters of 2 Chronicles 3, 4 and 5 the exact details of the temple are described in all its glory. Solomon truly wanted to build something spectacular for God.

You look at Solomon and the glorious temple he built for God, and think it would have been so easy for Solomon to take the credit, get a bit big for his britches and start to focus on his wealth instead of God. Yet when the temple is completed, and he was dedicating the temple, not once did he steal the limelight, he honours God in His rightful place and tells the people, they only have what they have and they are only where they are because of God. See 2 Chronicles 6.

That, my friend, takes character! Our history is littered with those who started out with good intentions and got caught up in the 'glory' of it and forgot what the real purpose was.

We often think to ourselves, if only I had a....... fill in the blanks. Most of us, if we are lacking in the financial department, want money to fill that, 'if only' blank. We then think of our 'if only' in terms of, "If I had money I could do this and that and have this and that." Very rarely do we stop and think how us having heaps can bless others!

Why is it that some are more financially blessed than others? Why is it that some people are so stinking rich but all they care about is more and more of what they can get for themselves? Surely, they don't deserve all that money?!

I don't have the answers honestly. Jesus tells us there will always be poor among us – but He commands us to look after them. See Matt 26:11, Deut 15:11.

Interestingly, when Jesus says in John 12:8, *⁸ You will always have the poor among you, but you will not always have me."* I think maybe He is saying, something like, "You can have all the money in the world and you can try and convince yourself that you are going to use it for others, but unless you put Me first, that money will own you." When you place your strength, future and value in how much you have, you will never really see Jesus.

Mother Teresa, saw her value in God, there were times in her life where she was abundantly blessed with money and fame – yet she gave it all away. She truly saw her value in God, not in things of the earth.

When I was younger in years and faith, I went through a phase in my life where I had enough to pretty well live comfortably. Money actually passed in out and of my hands easily. I had no real thought that this might go away. It did! The sad part is that when the money was there, and I could spend as I wished, on what I wished, I personally had no value. I had put all my security in my finances – not the one Who provided all my needs. It was not until I was dead broke and on my own with two small children did I realise that my value was not in money, or the ability to earn or lose it – but in God, the One who would see me through my darkest times.

I would like to say that I 'got it all together' after that, but alas, I didn't. Again, the money, not as much, but enough to live on, came. I turned towards the things of the earth and forgot about God! Gosh, I am so embarrassed to admit this now, but it is true.

I went on this roller-coaster of have and have not several times before I finally found my value in Christ.

Today, I am not financially rich, yet I am not poor. I have enough to meet my needs and then some to meet my desires. The difference this time – I don't see my value in things of earth. My value is firmly in the Hands of my Saviour, Jesus. Life is so much more rewarding.

Solomon had all a man could want and more, yet he was not so caught up in his position and wealth to forget Who gave it all to him – and just as simply, could take it all away. Solomon put his faith and future firmly in the hands of God. The temple in all its wonder was not meant to last forever, for only God lasts forever.

You may be in a financial bind, you might be like me – up and down and missing the point. I would be lying if I said you don't need money. We live in a world where money is the currency that puts food on our table and a roof over our head. I can assure you though, those things are fleeting in the big picture.

When you take your eyes off your earthly value and look towards the Creator of all – you may not win the lotto, or even immediately get out of debt. But I can tell you from my own experience, when you are down to nothing, the only way to look is up! Look up to the eyes of your Saviour and He will see you through.

Let's all live like Solomon – wanting only to be wise and caring enough to meet the needs of others for God's glory.

There is no Ezra 3:16

Nehemiah 3:16
(NLT)

16Next to him was Nehemiah son of Azbuk, the leader of half the district of Beth-zur. ~~He~~ rebuilt the wall from a place across from the tombs of David's family as far as the water reservoir and the ~~H~~ouse of the Warriors.

When you first read Nehemiah chapter 3, it is quite monotonous – each verse is describing how a person or persons are rebuilding a part of the wall around Jerusalem to fortify it against the enemy. It's pretty boring I must say. But it is in God's Word – so therefore there is a reason. The first thing that popped into my mind was "It takes a village".

Nehemiah chapter 3 has 32 verses that pretty much say the same thing, Joe Builder repaired this part and Bob Carpenter repaired this part and on and on it goes. Who cares, really?

Let me break it down as to what I saw as important about this verse (and chapter).

It really does take a village. Every person needs to be working together to achieve the same goal. If even one person was off in their direction of building that wall – there would have been a weakness – they would have been vulnerable to attack.

The people of Jerusalem were working together for one cause under the leadership of Nehemiah. He outlined what needed to be done and then delegated and directed who was to do what and how.

It must have been an almighty pre-match speech – because every member worked on their section and did what they needed to do to achieve the common goal. Protection against attack from the enemy.

I don't want to go where I am about to go, but when God plants a seed, you have to go with it. I'm about to get pretty politically incorrect. At least, sort of, as I am still legally allowed to do so.

The Church in the past few years has copped a flogging. There have been the issues in the Catholic church – most notable but, trust me, these issues have been happening in other denominations too.

Preachers of the Word seem to be so scared of teaching God's Holy Word that they have (to the majority) become 'feel good' preachers. Only discussing safe topics on how to be a better person. Not even how to be a better warrior for Christ.

We've recently had Father's Day and an advert that spoke of how mummy and daddy make a perfect team was removed from the airways, as it was deemed too political!

I personally haven't heard of any minister of God's church stand up and fight for that advert – we are supposed to be a unified body of Christ and yet we are so divided in so many areas. No wonder the enemy can attack – our walls have been breached. We as one body are not watching our section of the wall in unity with our brothers and sisters in Christ. We are too busy 'feeling good' and not getting our hands dirty to protect the Word of God.

I was wondering, in regard to Father's Day, how many church services got their hands dirty by discussing the sanctity of marriage? How many ministers were brave enough to stand on God's Word and say enough is enough? God designed man to be man and woman to be woman – if any person identifies as something else, then I am sorry, something somewhere in their psyche has gone wrong! Pure and Simple. The Creator of the universe did not, and I repeat, did not create humans to be trans anything. The only thing we could say is that we are trans-ient - from our earthly life to eternity.

There's an old saying, how do you boil a frog? One degree at a time. The theory is that if the water only changes a little bit at a time, the frog's body temperature will adjust as the temperature goes up and not notice it is starting to boil until too late.

This is our world! We have let things slide, we have accepted political correctness as something *okay, don't stress, what really does it matter that*: in the 80's women started wearing shoulder pads to look more masculine or that men got to wear pastels and more feminine colours. Who cares right? Or that women's hairstyles became more and more severe and men's styles became more easy, breezy? Or when the super models became straight up and down, and clothes just hung from them? These aren't problems, are they?

One degree hotter.

In Australia, we have introduced a program within our schools to supposedly counter bullying of people who are different. Sadly, it seems the demographic of who gets bullied has changed, not the act of bullying in itself.

One degree hotter.

Our walls are being breached and now the lines are so blurred about 'love' that even churches – God's Church – is arguing amongst itself.

One degree hotter.

The enemy has been whispering in the ears of man since the dawn of time, since Adam and Eve ate the apple.

Wealth, success, prestige, recognition are all the vices we crave. We especially love to be recognised – for us as individuals. Who really wants to be the person who is known as the tea lady at the local church. Really – don't we all want to be the star?

Do not kid yourself – the enemy is in our churches – he is in the playground; the government, families, work, your sports club, your social group.

We are in such a political time it is almost too much to share amongst friends whether you feel strongly about keeping marriage between a man and a woman. Goodness, your friend Betty might have a cousin, sister, brother, aunt, uncle or whomever who has chosen a different lifestyle.

One degree hotter.

The scary part is that the argument is for love – love whomever you please – is a good one. I even find myself agreeing. After all, who am I to stand in judgement of anyone?

I have absolutely no right to tell anyone who they can or can't love – and believe me I have no intentions of doing so.

The gate is open, the new is here, and we cannot undo what has now become. There are many things over the years that we, as humans, have got monumentally wrong. So, we use those arguments to allow our minds to be swayed – what could possibly go wrong with allowing people to express their love for each other by changing the marriage laws?

One degree hotter.

Jesus is love and I am 100% convinced He loves everyone equally. He loves the boy who identifies as a girl, or the man who is attracted to another man. He loves the girl who feels more loved by another woman than she ever could be by a man. He loves the person who feels they are a different race than that they were born. He loves the impure, the dirty, the rich, the poor, the saintly and the everyday person. But, this I will take to my grave – He cannot abide by the sin!

Because God is love – He sent His Son Jesus to the world to save us from ourselves.

The church is supposed to be the place where Jesus is the Head and He is able to delegate to His people how to keep the wall from being breached.

We as a world are getting one degree hotter every day.

We talk about love –*4 Love is patient and kind. Love is not jealous or boastful or proud 5 or rude. It does not demand its own way.*

It is not irritable, and it keeps no record of being wronged. ⁶ It does not rejoice about injustice but rejoices whenever the truth wins out. ⁷ Love never gives up, never loses faith, is always hopeful, and endures through every circumstance. 1 Corinthians 13:4-7(NLT)

Love is not bullying a person into your opinion. Love is not threatening to kill someone because they are speaking out against something they feel very strongly about. Love is not firing a person because they won't kow-tow to an agenda. Love is not keeping quiet, when you know in your heart, that something does not sit right. Love is not pushing yourself onto someone who is unable to defend themselves or has the ability to discern right from wrong.

This is a passionate subject for me. I am passionate about honouring God's Word and speaking out for what He has taught as Truth.

Finishing up, I told you I was going to go where it is not politically correct to do so. What all this has to do with our verse is – we need solid leadership – God. We need to work together for One purpose – God's Church. We need to be happy with the role He has chosen to give us to see His Plan come together to keep the enemy from our gates.

Job 3:16
(NIV)

16"Or why was I not hidden away in the ground like a stillborn child, like an infant who never saw the light of day?"

Wow!

What a full-on statement! I was looking at this verse and wondered how many times in my life, I have had similar thoughts – not quite so poetically – but still, there have been times in my life when I wished I had never been born. The pain I was enduring at the time seemed all encompassing and I was unable to see a light at the end of the tunnel.

I've always struggled with Job. I tend to lean towards the dramatic. I get an aching bone and my brain goes to bone cancer, I endure a cold too long and I must be terminal. If there is a way to dramatize a situation, I am there. So, Job scares me. I don't want to endure anymore hardship. I don't want to get so sick that I want to die – or even worse wish I had never been born.

I wish I could say that as I have grown in faith, these fears have gone away. They haven't – I am still fearful, I am still always waiting for the other shoe to drop and I am always playing out the worst-case scenario in my mind before I take action in anything. Yes, it is debilitating, yes, I pray for the faith I should have, not fear – yet fear seems to be my closest frenemy.

How do I reconcile my utter trust in God the Creator of the universe and my fear? I feel the fear and do it anyway. FEAR Facing Expectations that Aren't Real!

I have learned, over the years, that God goes before me, is with me and never leaves me. So even in my fear, He is with me. I have also come to accept I am me, He created me as I am, so my fear and anxiousness is not a surprise to Him.

As I continually hand over my fear to God in each and every situation, I find He gives me the courage to just do it. Flying is something that scares me. I'm not really scared of the crashing part, it is the 'stuck' part. I can't get out. I'm not in control. Yes, Control Freak 101, here! Those of us who deal with anxiety and fear are all control freaks. It gives us a sense that we can somehow foretell the outcome! Bah humbug – we know it isn't true, but it gives the mind a chance to catch up to the body.

Back to flying, I hate it. There is a story there, but I won't go into it now. Recently I flew to Melbourne – about a 2.5hr flight. Last time I went I was a sweating mess. This time I was at peace. I allowed God to take my fear and my control issue and let Him deal with it.

I didn't change – God changed me! I didn't control the situation – God used my fear as a chance for me to trust.

Job's situation didn't change until his attitude changed. He had to let go and let God. This, by the way, is my favourite saying – *let go and let God.* I know that there is not a single thing in this world I can control – doesn't stop me trying – but I know I cannot control anything. I have no right to question the Creator of the universe on anything – I do, but I know I shouldn't.

Each time I argue the point, God proves He is the answer. Every time I feel overwhelmed, He shows me peace. When I feel I can't get out of bed, He gives me strength. There is such a freedom in knowing that I don't have to *do*! God *does*! He set forth a path for my life – I just have to walk it. There is such a peace in knowing I am in the Arms of the Most High God and I cannot fall!

Jeremiah 29:11 (AMP) *For I know the plans and thoughts that I have for you,' says the Lord, 'plans for peace and well-being and not for disaster, to give you a future and a hope.*

There is no Psalm 3:16

Proverbs 3:16
(NIV)

¹⁶"Long life is in her right hand; in her left hand are riches and honour."

All we have to do is search wisdom quotes on the internet and we will find an abundance of humorous, uplifting, bold, slap-in-the-face quotes all sharing their opinion of wisdom.

Proverbs is full of wise quotes on how to live our lives. What does this mean though? Surely wisdom needs to be more than a plethora of inspirational words!

How do we get this wisdom to resonate? How do we bring this wisdom deep into our hearts, so we are changed from the inside?

Proverbs 3 is just so powerful.

It all comes back to allowing God to be the ruler of your heart and mind. Allowing Him to have the final say on the direction of your life and allowing His Words to penetrate deeply into your heart, mind and soul. When you meditate on the Words of wisdom

– the Words that God has put in simple, layman terms for us to follow – you will find peace, you will find freedom and you will find that this thing we call life is truly beautiful!

I have been thinking on this topic for the past few days and wondered what I could say. Truth is, I don't need to say anything- because God already has.

One thing I will say though, as you read the following scripture, there will be the odd one or two (maybe more) that will really hit home for you. Highlight them, print them out and put them somewhere so that you will be reminded daily.

Read through this wonderful piece of God's Word and allow it to get right into the nitty, gritty part of you. Live by these words and you will live a life you only ever dreamed of.

Proverbs 3 (AMP) The Rewards of Wisdom

1My son, do not forget my [a]teaching, but let your heart keep my commandments; 2For length of days and years of life [worth living] and tranquillity and prosperity [the wholeness of life's blessings] they will add to you.

3Do not let mercy and kindness and truth leave you [instead let these qualities define you]; bind them [securely] around your neck, write them on the tablet of your heart. 4So find favour and high esteem in the sight of God and man.

5Trust in and rely confidently on the Lord with all your heart and do not rely on your own insight or understanding.

6[b]In all your ways know and acknowledge and recognize Him, and He will make your paths straight and smooth [removing obstacles that block your way].

7Do not be wise in your own eyes; fear the Lord [with reverent awe and obedience] and turn [entirely] away from evil.

8It will be health to your body [your marrow, your nerves, your sinews, your muscles all your inner parts] and refreshment (physical well-being) to your bones. 9Honor the Lord with your wealth and with the first fruits of all your crops (income); 10Then your barns will be abundantly filled, and your vats will overflow with new wine. 11My son, do not reject or take lightly the discipline of the Lord [learn from your mistakes and the testing that comes from His correction through discipline]; nor despise His rebuke,

12For those whom the Lord loves He corrects, even as a father corrects the son in whom he delights.

13Happy [blessed, considered fortunate, to be admired] is the man who finds [skilful and godly] wisdom, and the man who gains understanding and insight [learning from God's word and life's experiences],

14For wisdom's profit is better than the profit of silver, and her gain is better than fine gold.

15She is more precious than rubies; and nothing you can wish for compares with her [in value].

16Long life is in her right hand; in her left hand are riches and honour.

17Her ways are highways of pleasantness and favour, and all her paths are peace.

18She is a tree of life to those who take hold of her, and happy [blessed, considered fortunate, to be admired] is everyone who holds her tightly.

19The Lord by His wisdom has founded the earth; by His understanding

He has established the heavens.

20By His knowledge the deeps were broken up and the clouds drip with dew.

21My son, let them not escape from your sight, but keep sound wisdom and discretion,

22And they will be life to your soul (your inner self) and a gracious adornment to your neck (your outer self).

23Then you will walk on your way [of life] securely and your foot will not stumble. 24When you lie down, you will not be afraid; when you lie down, your sleep will be sweet.

25Do not be afraid of sudden fear, nor of the storm of the wicked when it comes [since you will be blameless];

26For the Lord will be your confidence, firm and strong, and will keep your foot from being caught [in a trap].

27[c]Do not withhold good from those to whom it is due [its rightful recipients], when it is in your power to do it.

28Do not say to your neighbour, "Go, and come back, and tomorrow I will give it," when you have it with you.

29Do not devise evil against your neighbour, who lives securely beside you.

30Do not quarrel with a man without cause, if he has done you no harm.

31Do not envy a man of violence and do not choose any of his ways.

32For the devious are repulsive to the Lord; but His private counsel is with the upright [those with spiritual integrity and moral courage].

33 The curse of the Lord is on the house of the wicked, but He blesses the home of the just and righteous.

34 Though He scoffs at the scoffers and scorns the scorners, yet He gives His grace [His undeserved favour] to the humble [those who give up self-importance].

35 The wise will inherit honour and glory, but dishonour and shame is conferred on fools.

Prayer: *Precious Father, thank you for Your Word, thank you that you have given us such clear instruction on how to live a long, peaceful and fulfilled life. Help me, oh Lord, to take Your Word deep into my heart with every breath I take. For each breath is an undeserved gift from You. In all things, in all ways, Father we give you the glory. Amen*

Ecclesiastes 3:16
(AMP)

16 Moreover, I have seen under the sun that in the place of justice there is wickedness, and in the place of righteousness there is wickedness.

Most people know this chapter, or at least the first eight verses, due to the very popular rendition by *The Byrds – Turn! Turn! Turn! (To Everything There is a Season)*. Yes, you are probably humming it to yourself now.

What of the verse at hand today? From verse nine, Ecclesiastes seems to lay the foundation that everything is not as it should be here on earth and that this is just a waiting place for us to be until we die. He almost appears to be totally melancholy about the whole deal of life. *'What's the point anyway, man just keeps stuffing it up, so you might as well try and make the most of the time you have here, because who knows what happens next!'*

As Christians, we talk about the end days, the return of Jesus. It seems that every generation since Jesus ascended to Heaven has believed they are in the 'final end-times' and therefore Jesus would return in their lifetime.

We read God's Word and try to interpret it to the best of our ability and read the signs and wonders to convince ourselves that our generation is the worst, the best, the last and so on. Yet, generation after generation, here we are. There are many variants on who wrote, and when, Ecclesiastes was written, but to say it has been narrowed down to somewhere between 450 BC and 180 BC, which basically means a long time ago.

Our verse is full of doom and gloom – we could read this verse and go, 'yep, this is where we are at' If we saw this written by a modern-day inspirational leader, we would be getting our bags ready for the final trip home.

We are living in an ugly time in history, yet if we ask generations before, they would say, theirs was an ugly time, and they would be right.

So, as Ecclesiastes says, what is the point?

Jesus is the point! He came, He conquered, He set us free. We do not need to live in the bondage of what is going to happen next. Or stress about when He is going to return, or when God is going to wipe out the world and start again with the new Earth! In the big scheme of things these are unimportant.

How can we live in the freedom of Christ if we are always waiting for the shoe to drop?! How can we really live in relationship with Jesus if we are always trying to figure out the legalism of the Bible? How can we truly live, *'Your will be done, on earth as it is in heaven'* if we are always wondering when He is going to come back and take us home?

I know as Christians, we need to live as if we are already at home with Jesus, but how can we show the love of Christ if we have one foot out the door?

Those who do not know Jesus don't need to think about the end of the world, they are living in the darkness already. Why would we, who are trying to reflect Love, make it even more scary? Yes, once we know Christ, we understand that His return is a good thing, but to others it is not.

I personally think, and scholars may argue, that we need to reflect Christ here! In our everyday. We need to be living our life as if Jesus were here right now! Live how He lived. Embrace life, live each moment with true love and passion and completeness of this life. By doing this, we, in turn, will reflect the life to come.

I see those in this life who profess to be born again Christians and they are absolute sad-sacks. This is not what Jesus wants for us. He wants us to live life with a smile on our dial and a leap in our hearts. He wants us to laugh, sing, dance and embrace life as if He is the only one watching.

Take time out of your busy lives, try and find the tiniest flower you can and wonder in its perfection. Watch an ant go about its business, sit and watch children play in the park. Watch the old man feed the birds. Stand in the rain or catch a snow flake on your tongue. Smile at a stranger, so hello as you pass by. Smile at all times, get people wondering what is going on.

Embrace your challenges as a chance to learn and grow and then teach others. Submerge yourself in the little things that make you smile, so they are a reflection of who you are.

Let the love of Christ and His very being ooze out of every pore of your being.

Let us embrace the Lord's prayer found in Matthew 6:9-13. Below is my interpretation:

Our Precious Father, who stands in the Heavens and yet is everywhere, Your name is the highest and most awesome name and may we remember that!

Let Your Kingdom come, let Your Will be done – here on earth, where you have placed us to be, your children, and show the world Your Love and what Heaven will be like, because we will be living it, reflecting it, here, now.

Give us each day what we need, so that we don't have to have stress – so we can show people just what being in a relationship with you is all about.

Forgive us each time we stuff up, cause let's face it, we do it daily, possibly hourly. Then, with this forgiveness, help us to forgive others as You forgave us – completely!

Help keep us on the straight and narrow path that leads to You, so that by the way we live, others will see You and want what we have. Keep us protected from the enemy, so that we don't walk into the temptations of this life and by doing so drag others down with us.

Everything is Yours, everything we have or think we own is because of You, and when we fully grasp this Lord, we will fully understand just what You have given us. We will then understand the might and majesty of just saying Your name. For it means - All power, All glory, is Yours. Amen

Isaiah 3:16
(NIV)

16The LORD says, "The women of Zion are haughty, walking along with outstretched necks, flirting with their eyes, strutting along with swaying hips, with ornaments jingling on their ankles.

As a woman, I hate seeing women as the villain in a movie or the one who brings ruin to her family or to her husband. It seems so foreign to me that women can be bad.

I like to think of women as soft, caring, loving and the one who holds the family together. I guess I like to believe that every woman can be, or is, the Proverbs woman found in 31:10-31.

It seems, though, that what God designed to be good and beautiful, the enemy set out to destroy.

Sadly, the more I delve into God's Word, I discover that women can be evil. They can be the undoing of many a good man and they can bring nations to their knees. It was a woman who wanted

John the Baptist's head (Matt 14), Delilah, who brought Samson to his knees (Judges 16), Potiphar's wife who accused Joseph of rape (Gen 39), and Jezebel, who was just downright evil (1 Kings 18) – to name a few.

God created us to be soft, yet strong; wise, yet humble; a caretaker and a nurturer. He gave us the toughest job around – to bring another life into the world. He gifted us, in a way, that we are able to guide a man on the path he should go, when he is a bit lost and confused as to how he should be moving forward in his life. History is filled with stories of men who have fallen and in their last breaths they call for their mother or their wife. They want to let them know that they love them, that they hope they made them proud, that they stood tall for them.

Please don't get me wrong, I am far from a barefoot, pregnant and stuck in the kitchen kind of woman. I am a director of a company, I run my own business, I have raised my children to be good, kind and beautiful people. I am argumentative to the core and I will stand my ground when I believe there has been injustice. I do not believe that God made woman weak – I believe the exact opposite.

So, how do we avoid becoming the woman described in Isaiah 3:16? How do we live a life of honour towards God and be who He created us to be? How do we distinguish ourselves apart from man, yet be a part of him?

In John 4, the Samaritan woman is at the well, here she meets Jesus, who tells her who she is and what she has done in her life. She had two options, she could have abused Jesus and told him to shove it and continue with her life – it had, after all, been all she had known. Or, as is the case, she could take His Words into her heart and change her life. Her life changing experience with the Messiah, actually made her the first evangelist! She told everyone, *'come, see the man who told me everything I have ever done'*.

To answer the questions, Jesus is the answer!

Allow Him to enter your heart, your mind and your very being. Through Him, you can become the woman you were created to be. As women, we have a massive responsibility – we cannot take this lightly.

We can choose to be the downfall of men, or we can choose to be the vessel that God created to guide, care and love mankind. We start with our siblings, then our male friends, then our husband and then our children (or the children God has placed in our path).

In living as God intended, we do not lose self, we find self! I didn't always understand this, I thought giving into God meant becoming a doormat. I've now realised just how influential a woman of God can be. I am stronger and freer than I have ever known.

I've stepped into the woman God created me to be.

Choose today, to allow God to show you your flaws. Let Him reveal all the things you have done. Be like the Samaritan woman, embrace it, find the love for self that you may never have known and go into your world and share who you really are. A precious child of the Living God!

Jeremiah 3:16
(NLT)

> 16"And when your land is once more filled with people," says the LORD, "you will no longer wish for 'the good old days' when you possessed the Ark of the LORD's Covenant. You will not miss those days or even remember them, and there will be no need to rebuild the Ark.

Have you ever wanted to go back and re-watch a movie or tv show from your childhood? With Netflix and all the extra channels on the tv, quite often this is possible. Once you've seen it though, are you sorely sorry you didn't leave the past where it was? What you remembered wasn't quite as good as it seemed to be.

Now my theory on this is, that at the time of watching our childhood tv show or movie, the technology surrounding that time was the best it could be – for that time! Compared to technology today, of course it pales into comparison. But! At the time when we first watched, that was the way it was, that's the way it was done and we loved it. That's why we often wish 'we could go back'. Go back to a 'better, quieter, peaceful, easier time' – they are our memories. They are not necessarily the facts.

In Jeremiah's time, and let's face it, throughout the Bible, man has walked away from God and has only come back when the messy stuff hit the fan.

God, through Jeremiah is saying, pure and simple – I'm sick of you pretending to come back to me. I'm sick of you holding onto idols and looking for tangibles to hold.

God says – "I AM! I am enough – you don't need the past to back Me up, you don't need "things" to remind you I am here. You don't need to go back and watch re-runs. The re-runs are a part of your journey yes, they served a purpose for the time and the audience they were speaking to. My Word will stand forever, but what man has done is not a true representation of Me. (Taking liberties here of speaking for God)"

God is beyond words gracious, kind, loving, forgiving and above all Love! He shows us over and over again that there is absolutely nothing we, as His people, can do to make Him turn His back on us. Throughout the Word of God, His ultimate message is – I LOVE YOU! He gets mad, He punishes us for our misbehaviour, He takes away our toys and He makes us accountable for our actions. This though, is the ultimate show of Love. If we love our children then we love them, punish them for their misadventures and try to guide them on the right path. We look at society today and think – 'if only parents took the role of parenting more seriously and disciplined their children, maybe things wouldn't be so bad.'

Well, that is what God has been doing, will continue to do and will never stop doing – until Jesus' return.

I think that He is trying to tell us – "stop looking for Me in things, stop trying to make up the rules as you go along. I've shown you, I sent you My Son as the ultimate tangible of what LOVE looks like. You don't need an ark, you don't need crosses with a crucified Jesus on it or symbols of religion. I AM in the very breath you breathe, the creator of the gentle breeze, the trees, the grass, the wind, the rain. I AM in every cell in your being.

'Reach into you! Look for Me, I am there – waiting; loving you. For if I am a part of you – how can you ever, ever be without me?! I say, I will never leave you or forsake you. I cannot lie, I cannot be untrue to myself. Give up the 'things' – turn to Me the Creator of all things. I will not let you down!

Lamentations 3:16
(NIV)

16 "He has broken my teeth with gravel; he has trampled me in the dust."

Do we as people ever learn? I am thinking, as a whole, the answer appears to be no.

As a Christian, I am heartbroken at our world. I, as an individual, am also powerless to do anything other than pray to God that He keeps His promise that the ultimate victory is His.

I am not sure how bad things will get in my lifetime, but I feel that it is getting pretty bad as it is.

I remember listening to a Shane Willard devotional and he was talking about when he counsels people, quite often the question they ask is, "How did this happen to me?"

Shane goes on to say, tongue in cheek, "Oh, what, you woke up this morning and your marriage was just over?" Or, "Seriously, you went to your back account and there was money in it yesterday, but today there is zero in it?"

The point he was trying to make is – things very rarely, 'just happen', there are a series of events that lead to the crunch in our lives where we 'hit rock bottom' and realise something is wrong.

As harsh as it sounds, we actually are getting what we deserve.

I remember as a young woman I had made some monstrous miscalculations in my life. Truth be told, my rebellious streak throughout my entire childhood and young adult life, led to those choices. Some of those choices were made out of pure stubborn pride, which led me down a path of destruction. I would scream out to God to fix it, why was this happening, how could He ignore me in a time like this?

I hit rock bottom and all I had left was to look up! Now, that would be lovely if that was the end of it. If only God looked at me, and said, 'Kerrilee, good on you, you've realised the errors of your ways, it is smooth sailing here on out.'

This part of the lesson was tough, I had repented, I had laid my heart bare, I had turned my life around – Why. Was. It. All. Still. Crap?

My beautiful mother explained to me, you reap what you sow. I didn't quite get this until I realised what is involved with planting a crop.

Prepare the soil – this is either done well or poorly. Depending how well you lay the foundations here, will have a massive impact on how well your crop will grow.

Take care in the way you plant – if you follow the guidelines, and those who have gone before you (who have succeeded) you will have a better chance at a good crop. If you scatted seeds wherever you feel like it and 'do it your way', your crop will fail.

Tend to your field – farmers watch over their crops as a mother watches over her young. Any sign of things heading in the wrong direction, the good farmer is out there sorting it out. If he doesn't have the answers, he seeks them from those who know.

Watch and harvest at the right time – a good farmer knows exactly when to plant, and to harvest. If you do not make sure the previous steps are taken care of – your crop will be full of weeds, the plants will be undernourished, and they may not be ready when it is time to reap the harvest.

Now, I sort of got these steps. I realised I had not been a good farmer of my life, I had taken the 'Kerrilee way' and not the God way. I still couldn't understand why it didn't all turn around again after the harvest.

That is when I realised, when the soil is poorly tended, the seeds of weeds and pestilence run deep. When a good farmer gets to the end of the season, he rests his field. He allows it time to rejuvenate. This is why there are some fields that are empty during a season – these fields are resting. They need time to repair from the damage of sustaining a crop. They need time for nutrients to be replaced. From the surface these fields look unkempt and unloved, yet the farmer is watching, learning, and preparing for when it is time to plant the good crop.

When we have reaped our harvest, our hearts, minds and body need to rest, rejuvenate and learn from the disaster of our last crop. If our previous 'crop' was poorly tended, there is a lot of work to do to get our lives back to a place of fresh beginnings.

I know, from personal experience, the road back to no longer dealing with the 'old crop' takes time – oh my goodness does it take time. This is where I know a lot of people give up, walk away and think God is not listening or caring.

The truth is, we are exactly where He said we would end up, if we continued on the path we set in motion.

God cannot lie, He cannot go against His own Word. This doesn't mean He doesn't cry with us or feel our pain as we traverse this thing called life. He, like the good farmer, is watching, waiting, tending in the background so that when we have run the course, and learned from our past, He can help us to plant the next crop.

The exciting thing about reaping what you sow, a good crop, gets good return!

Ezekiel 3:16
(NIV)

16"At the end of seven days the Word of the Lord came to me:"

When God gets hold of you, there really isn't too much you can do to prevent His Word being filled.

Isaiah 55:11 (CEV) *"That's how it is with my Words. They don't return to Me without doing everything I send them to do."*

This devotional is several years in the making, but God is persistent and so here I am. My prayer is that I do Him justice with the words that flow.

Ezekiel was called to be as hard and bull-headed as the Israelites he was sent to reach. God made Ezekiel tough enough to handle their rebuke. He filled his heart with the Word of God so that there would be an undeniable passion to share the Words he had been called to share.

Then, there was a time of waiting! Ugh waiting! That is the worst part, isn't it?!

Why does God give us a vision, a purpose, a reason and then put the brakes on? Can't we just go in, guns a blazin', mouth going at 100 miles an hour? After all, aren't we armed with the Word of God and can conquer everything?

I think the time of waiting is preparation. I think we have to allow the Words to seep into our hearts so deep that no matter what the opposition we will stand fast and steady.

I'm not sure if any men reading this will get this part, but I am pretty sure every woman will. Women rehearse our speech, we run through the scenario a dozen (or more) times in all different angles so that when we are ready move, we feel prepared, ready and able to handle all different responses and reactions we may receive.

The times that we go in 'guns a blazin' and mouth at 100 miles an hour' – well they are the times where it all falls apart and we end up wondering whether we have a valid case or not.

Time = confidence

Time = readiness

Time = steadfastness

Ezekiel was to be held accountable for his next step. If he chose not to face the Israelites and tell them all that God placed on his heart, which was pretty full-on, I might add, he was told that he is responsible for their blood. See Ezekiel 3:18

That's a pretty heavy thing to place on someone, so imagine not being ready! Ezekiel had to face these people who probably would have rather thrown stones at him than listen to what he had to say.

God knew that Ezekiel had to be ready. He had to be tough

physically, mentally, emotionally and spiritually before he entered the 'ring'.

So, He made him wait!

We do not have the advantage, like many of those from the Old Testament who audibly heard God speak. They had a clear direction of what He wanted. But goodness, even those who heard him often didn't wait, and went about doing things their own way. So, be kind to yourself when you are frustrated with the waiting, unsure if you are waiting or procrastinating or even on the right path. Like me with this devotional, I knew what God wanted, for He gently showed me little signs as I procrastinated. His Word will not return void!

I am a person of action, I am not patient, and I hate inactivity. I'm also scared of not getting it right, thus the procrastination with getting this devotional started. Boy, God has a lot of work to do in me. But, when I wait, (not procrastinate) listen and pray, then all falls into place, the rewards are beyond measure.

Part of being obedient to God is not having to know why or what the waiting will bring, or if the waiting is even for us. Sometimes our waiting if for someone else.

Our job is to be open, ready and willing and yes, most of the time this means... we wait!

Daniel 3:16
(NIV)

16"Shadrach, Meshach and Abednego replied to him, "King Nebuchadnezzar, we do not need to defend ourselves before you in this matter."

Imagine being so confident in your faith that you could tell the King that you would not obey his command, as his command contradicted the Word of God! Wow! These guys were hard-core. They were so in love with God that they were prepared to die rather than worship another god.

When did you last compromise?

Maybe you haven't intentionally disobeyed God's Word, or even thought that you had compromised. I can assure you though, if you have a heartbeat, at some stage in your life, probably even in this last week or maybe even today, you have compromised.

God blows my mind, initially I had thought that the direction of this devotional would go a certain way, alas, God has had other ideas. So, stick with me while we take a turn. This is dedicated to women (sorry guys, I need to do this one just for us).

Lately, God has placed on my heart,

'You are who you associate with and what your thought patterns are!'.

I've been churning this around now for weeks. My Bible readings have reinforced this, my conversations have reinforced this, and my thought life has concreted this.

Compromise! I have had a hard look at myself and shamefully, I admit, more of my life than I would like to admit has been – compromise.

Ok, here we go, my list:

Gossiped – now I have not wanted to admit this, I've tried to justify that it is frustration that has led me to speak about another person in the ways I have.

You are who you associate with and what your thought patterns are! Ugh!

If I have an issue with someone, I should go to them, explain my frustrations – accept the consequences and move on. If the person continues to be toxic to my life. I MOVE ON! I should not keep sharing my frustrations with anyone who will listen.

Puffed myself up – I mean that I have made out that my life is just so darn important and busy that I couldn't possibly have time to deal with the 'little things' in life.

I have come to realise that this has been my own insecurity. We live in such a competitive world that if we are not 'better', busier or 'more' than someone else, well, we just aren't enough.

I am enough – I am the created child of the Almighty God. Made exactly the way He intended me to be! THAT IS ENOUGH!

Disrespected others and myself – example, when I don't want to do something, I deliberately make myself late or excuses as to why I just simply can't get here or there or be this or that. This might not seem important really, but it is – I am disrespecting the other person or people by thinking my arriving, or not arriving when I choose is okay. It is not. I don't like it being done to me, yet I find it okay to do to others. Eek!

My choice – admit I don't want to go and let the people know. Or, accept that it is something I need to do, (for whatever reason), show my respect and turn up on time.

This brings us back to - *You are who you associate with and what your thought patterns are!*

If the reason you do not want to go is the person or people are not good for your soul – then admit it, cut the ties and move on.

Said I am just a mum! – My heart breaks now when I think of this. I was, for most of my children's years, a stay-at-home mum. In my heart it was the best 'job' in the world. Yet to the world, I was too ashamed to admit that. I thought the world wanted more from me. I had to be this busy person always with a plan, a goal, a 'something', that was more than being just a mum. I needed to justify what I was doing with my life, who I was and why, someone like me, with my skills, was only a mum.

There is such a stigma in being a mum. If you work, you are persecuted, if you stay home you are looked down on. If you try to do both, well you are just flippant and not dedicated enough to do both.

I wanted to please the masses. I put on a different persona according to whom I mixed. Yet, very rarely, did I just accept that I was exactly where God placed me to be, and that was to be the very best mum I could be for the children He had entrusted me with.

You are who you associate with and what your thought patterns are! Ouch!

Trust me, I could go on, but I am feeling heavy hearted enough with admitting these things.

As a woman, and I am sure as a man (yet I am not one, so can't say for certain) we spend far too much of our lives being what others want us to be. Only issue with that, every person has a different idea of who that 'someone' should be.

Every day, in little ways, we compromise who we are to please others. We go where we don't want to go, we say what we don't want to say, we act in ways we do not want to, and we listen to and associate with people who we know are not healthy for us. We allow people to prevent us from moving forward with our lives.

We compromise. We do not stand true to who God created us to be. We do not find that peace and solitude in just 'being'. We constantly feel, in this fast-moving world, that we must be doers, not 'be'ers.

I think, in many ways, 99% of us, do not even know who we are!

Psalm 139:14 *"I praise you because I am fearfully and wonderfully made; your works are wonderful, I know that full well."*

Romans 12:2 *"Do not conform to the pattern of this world, but be transformed by the renewing of your mind. Then you will be able to test and approve what God's will is—his good, pleasing and perfect will."*

Victoria Osteen *"When God created you, He went to great lengths to make you exactly the way He wanted you to be. You are His ultimate work of art."*

Question for today: If you were in Shadrach, Meshach and Abednego's position, would you know who you are well enough to stand firm?

Thought for today: Once you choose and know who you are in Christ, your past no longer defines you, it belongs to God, He took it when Jesus went to the cross. God chooses to take your shameful, painful past and throw it into the abyss – never to be seen again. God gave you a clean slate when you said – Jesus is my saviour – start writing your new story today!

And kiss compromise goodbye forever!

There is no ~~Hosea~~ 3:16

Joel 3:16
(NIV)

16" The LORD will roar from Zion and thunder from Jerusalem; the earth and the heavens will tremble. But the LORD will be a refuge for his people, a stronghold for the people of Israel."

I am no Bible scholar, but I am aware that a common thread throughout the Old Testament is God's judgement. God's chosen people the Israelites, I believe, took God for granted. They were, what we call in the industry, classic abusers. At some level they were so certain that it didn't really matter what they did, because they are God's 'chosen', so He will eventually forgive them, re-set and they could carry on. Sadly, even to today, the Jewish nation is waiting for their Saviour.

As a 'gentile' I am eternally grateful for the Cross! I am eternally grateful that Jesus opened the door to those of us who were not the 'chosen' people.

Acts 26:23 (NLT) *"that the Messiah would suffer and be the first to rise from the dead, and in this way, announce God's light to Jews and Gentiles alike."*

As a gentile, I am not immune against the *"God will forgive me for my behaviour"* mentality. My life has been a series of ups and downs, of walking with God and walking my own path.

I love how Joel starts off with, 'this is what will happen if you continue on the path you are going.' He is like – *'Can't you get it through your thick heads that God is the God of LOVE; He wants for you what no other in all the universe can do for you!'* Yet he always finishes with – *'This is how wonderful it will be if you turn back to God and live your life according to His will and purpose.'*

God cannot lie, He cannot be untrue to Himself and He is a just God. So, when we sin, we must be aware that there are consequences for our actions.

I look at our world today and I see that there really are no consequences for bad behaviour. Our sporting heroes get caught up in their fast-paced, ever demanding world and they make a mistake – they are slapped on the wrist and move on. Our children are watching this!

Our public figures portrayed in the media, do as they please, 'ask for forgiveness after the fact' – our children are watching this!

Movies and TV shows are full of 'live life how you want, darn the consequences' – our children are watching this!

Parents have abdicated their responsibility of true parenting and they blame the education system, the lack of finances, the way they were raised and so on. Our children are watching this!

The education system has given up all sense of discipline – it is all about 'love and acceptance' yet it is really just full of hatred and 'do whatever feels good' mentality. Our children are living this!

God is watching this!

God though, is the God of LOVE – He sent His Son Jesus! God sent the ultimate sacrifice for our sins. We do not have to live as the world lives, we do not have to conform to the way the 'world' justifies its behaviour.

Romans 12:2 AMP *"And do not be conformed to this world [any longer with its superficial values and customs], but be transformed and progressively changed [as you mature spiritually] by the renewing of your mind [focusing on godly values and ethical attitudes], so that you may prove [for yourselves] what the will of God is, that which is good and acceptable and perfect [in His plan and purpose for you]."*

Because of Jesus, we have a choice. We have the benefit of all of God's Word written before us. We have a reminder every year of exactly what Jesus did for us.

All of God's judgement for the world fell on Jesus' shoulders.

He took the burdens, the sin, the hatred, the despicable things mankind does to each other and took that to the cross.

He left it there when He rose again.

His resurrection is why, we can be free today.

The harsh judgement of Joel and other Old Testament verses have been superseded by Jesus' Love. This does not mean we can carry on in our sinful nature and live a carefree life – it means there is an easy way to move from this world's thinking and behaviour to the love and Grace of God. and it's through Jesus,

There is no Amos, Jonah or Micah 3:16

Nahum 3:16
(NIV)

16"You have increased the number of your merchants till they are more numerous than the stars in the sky, but like locusts they strip the land and then fly away."

Have we, as people, changed from those of the Old Testament? Have we come closer to what God expects from His Creation?

Sadly, I believe the answer is no.

We can read the Old Testament and wonder how they got it all so wrong, but gosh, let's just look at our world today!

We are on a path of self-destruction. We are drawing ever closer to the time that God will send Jesus back and that will be the end of what we know as our 'Earth'

As a Christian, this should not be a cause for concern, in fact, this should be a cause for celebration. Knowing that God fulfils His promises – His Word. The Holy Bible is full of His fulfilled promises. So, as Christians, we know, that on the day that Jesus

Christ returns for His people, we are to be counted among that number.

We can't go through our lives just waiting for the day Jesus returns and forget about living here. We have a job to do and that is to reach those who do not yet know Him. We are called to love, that is to LOVE, with capitals. Not when we feel like it or want to, but always.

God is the same yesterday, today and He will be the same tomorrow. He has the whole thing mapped out and as history shows, He continually offers His people (that is, every human who has ever walked the face of this planet) a way to repent, change their ways and follow His path. Time and time again though, mankind foopoohs in God's face and does things in the 'feels good, so I'll do it mentality'. God wants more, He deserves more, and we should want to give Him more.

Everything here that God placed on this planet is for us to enjoy. Yet we are systematically destroying this world. The people in our lives are here to help us learn love, yet we back-bite, argue and crush each other for our own selfish gain.

No, the people who walk the Earth today, are no different to the people who walked the Earth in the Old Testament.

Even though we don't see God flooding the Earth, sending plagues of locusts or destroying nations, doesn't mean we don't deserve it!

We, as a people in general, have walked away from God, we have spat in His face and even said He doesn't exist.

As His children though, we have a responsibility to live our lives for Him. To live our every waking moment in such a way that others cannot help but see there is something different about us.

We must not walk the walk of the average man.

Through our actions we must reflect the purest LOVE of Christ. We don't have to defend God, we don't have to get into arguments trying to prove a point. We just need to LOVE our neighbours as we are supposed to love ourselves. We learn to love ourselves by allowing Jesus to LOVE us. When we accept His LOVE, we can love ourselves and thus love others.

When we show LOVE, others cannot help but to want what we have!

Habakkuk 3:16
(NET)

16I listened and my stomach churned; the sound made my lips quiver. My frame went limp, as if my bones were decaying, and I shook as I tried to walk. I long for the day of distress to come upon the people who attack us.

Have you ever been so afraid of something that you can relate to the words above from Habakkuk?

I know I have!

In my life I have had experiences where I truly did not think I was going to make it out the other side. Fear overwhelmed me.

Interestingly, in the moment of the extreme, fear is not an issue – adrenalin kicks in and you go into auto-pilot. For me, my 'go-to' is freeze momentarily and then I fight! I've always been a fighter, just ask my mum.

Fear comes either before, or, now this is the surprising part, *after* the actual event!

The lead up to an event, that we see as daunting, causes us to create pictures in our minds of what could happen. Then after the fact, we start to think about what could have happened and start to think, if it happened once, it could happen again. This kind of fear leads to anxiety which is incredibly detrimental to our health.

When I was young, I learnt a little saying – FEAR – **F**acing **E**xperiences that **A**ren't **R**eal! Don't get me wrong, I learnt it, but haven't always implemented it.

More times than not, our fear is unwarranted. It is our mind that conjures up all the worst-case scenarios.

In Habakkuk, the fear he is talking about is the impending doom of being attacked. It happened – they were in a terrible state. They had nothing left. Why, then, was he singing songs of praise, when he knew the worst was yet to come?

He put his trust in God.

Every moment of every day we are given a chance to choose between trusting in God or trusting in the world.

A scripture that is fast becoming my go-to is

2 Cor 5:7 (NIV) *For we live by faith, not by sight*

If we live our lives based on what we see around us, we would be in a constant state of fear. Our bodies would literally start to break down due to the constant surge of adrenalin that courses through our veins.

I, by nature, am anxious. I have had debilitating panic attacks. I have a creative mind, so I am always imagining the worst that could happen. To be honest, each day can be a battle to even leave the house.

Those who know me well, get this, those who don't, can't believe I am that person!

I put it down to putting my trust in God, allowing the Holy Spirit to dwell within me and putting the armour on every single day. I love this version from the Amplified Bible.

Ephesians 6:10-18 (AMP)

10 In conclusion, be strong in the Lord [draw your strength from Him and be empowered through your union with Him] and in the power of His [boundless] might. 11 Put on the full armor of God [for His precepts are like the splendid armor of a heavily-armed soldier], so that you may be able to [successfully] stand up against all the schemes and the strategies and the deceits of the devil. 12 For our struggle is not against flesh and blood [contending only with physical opponents], but against the rulers, against the powers, against the world forces of this [present] darkness, against the spiritual forces of wickedness in the heavenly (supernatural) places. 13 Therefore, put on the complete armor of God, so that you will be able to [successfully] resist and stand your ground in the evil day [of danger], and having done everything [that the crisis demands], to stand firm [in your place, fully prepared, immovable, victorious]. 14 So stand firm and hold your ground, having tightened the wide band of truth (personal integrity, moral courage) around your waist and having put on the breastplate of righteousness (an upright heart), 15 and having strapped on your feet the gospel of peace in preparation [to face the enemy with firm-footed stability and the readiness produced by the good news]. 16 Above all, lift up the [protective] shield of faith with which you can extinguish all the flaming arrows of the evil one. 17 And take the helmet of salvation, and the sword of the Spirit, which is the Word of God.

> 18 With all prayer and petition pray [with specific requests] at all times [on every occasion and in every season] in the Spirit, and with this in view, stay alert with all perseverance and petition [interceding in prayer] for all God's people.

I still get afraid, I still want to freeze and then fight – yet now I do it with the help of the Holy Spirit. My gut still churns, my heart still races, and I still pray that whatever I am imaging could happen won't!

But like Habakkuk I need to be prepared that the worst-case may eventuate. The news I am waiting on really is bad, the person I am praying for does not get well. The money dries up, the job is lost and on and on it goes.

Human nature means we become fearful – it is instinctual – yet we don't have to make it habitual. We can accept we are afraid and then hand it to God. We can allow Him to bring us the peace beyond all understanding.

Philipians 4:7 (NLT) *Then you will experience God's peace, which exceeds anything we can understand. His peace will guard your hearts and minds as you live in Christ Jesus.*

Next time fear comes-a-knockin, open the door wearing God's armour – you will be surprised to find that fear is no longer there!

Zephaniah 3:16
(AMP)

16In that day it will be said to Jerusalem: "Do not be afraid, O Zion; Do not let your hands fall limp.

Have you ever been so angry with someone you loved that you thought, this is it! I cannot fathom ever getting over this anger, hurt and frustration? Their every action, in your opinion, felt as if they were just doing everything in their power to 'dig-the-knife in'. You have shed burning tears of heartache and frustration, wondering if the bond can ever be restored. Bitter words are spoken, and even more bitter ones are thought. That's it, there is no going back, they've gone too far this time! Your whole body goes limp at the sense of defeat of it all.

Then,

A simple gesture, a word, a look and all is forgiven!

The cavern of despair is closed, the heartache is gone. Gone so much in fact, you almost can't even remember why there was so much angst in the first place.

Now think on this, we are fallible humans and we get angry over things that affect us. We get angry over differing opinions, hurt feelings, that people aren't doing what we believe to be the right course of action. Yet, in reality, who says that our opinion is correct? It is all a matter of perspective isn't it. Arguments evolve for we, both sides, are determined to be right. Seems kind of petty when we put it like that, but that is reality of it. If one party is okay with not having to prove their point – the argument has no fuel.

Mankind, since Adam and Eve, have been trying to prove they are right. The Bible is a living documentary of the arguments between man and God. Man trying to be right – God is RIGHT! Man fighting to be supreme – God is SUPREME! When you are dealing with the Creator of everything – how could man ever be right? But every day, we witness mankind trying to be right and prove God wrong.

We have witnessed, through His Holy Word, that there have been times when God has reigned fire on mankind's silly butt. He has disciplined, rebuked, punished and even, all but wiped out every last human. Unlike our frustration with our loved ones, He has the right to do all this. His anger is just, ours is just selfish. His anger is out of pure love for us, our anger is out of wanting to be heard. His anger is for our benefit, our anger is for our recognition.

We can read over the Bible and think, yeah, they got what they deserved, God should have wiped them out, He should have carried out His threats to punish them. Yet, we notice time and time again that God sees a simple gesture, a word, a look – all is forgiven!

We are no different to the generations of people throughout the Word of God – we are just as sinful, selfish, self-willed, arrogant and determined to be right. We deserve His punishment. Yet, through His Son, Jesus Christ, we have salvation, we have forgiveness.

Every time we lose our tempers towards the ones we love and then forgive them just as quick, we are seeing the Love of God through our actions. We can only love and forgive others, because He loved and forgave us first.

Next time you feel that fire of frustration welling up inside of you, think carefully, what is the cause of your anger – is it justified, or do you just want to be right?

When you are considering not forgiving someone for their actions against you – remember that God forgave you, even though you have never really deserved it.

And when you are determined to be right, to win the argument, what is the price you could pay? Is being right worth winning an argument, but losing love?

Thank you God that You see value in us. Thank you that we are Your Greatest Creation and that Your anger towards us is justified. Thank you, God, that Your LOVE supersedes all the anger. Thank you Precious Father that in Your Love you sent Your Son Jesus as our Compass back to You. Amen.

There is no Haggai or Zechariah 3:16

Malachi 3:16
(MSG)

> 16 Then those whose lives honored God got together and talked it over. God saw what they were doing and listened in. A book was opened in God's presence and minutes were taken of the meeting, with the names of the God-fearers written down, all the names of those who honored God's name.

We are about to close out the Old Testament. The Old Testament to me, as a child, was the part of the Bible I tried to ignore. I didn't like the doom and gloom of it all. I liked the New Testament with the love of Jesus part.

As I've grown, and especially since embarking on this journey of trying to capture 3:16's for God, I have learned that the Old Testament is all about Jesus. It is all about the Love of God and preparing the world for Jesus's coming to Earth.

Yes, there really is a lot of doom and gloom in the Old Testament, but that is because the people did not understand relationship with God. They saw Him as this distant unobtainable deity who they could never aspire to be like, nor would they have ever considered to be 'God-like'. Maybe they wanted to be 'gods in their own right', but, never could they comprehend to be the One True God – for they simply did not understand Him. He was in the sky, distant, in a box, contained, or in a temple; separated. He was not flesh and blood who walked among them and felt their pain.

Old Testament time was full of gods. Each one supposedly promising wealth and wonders, health and harmony. Each god, ultimately letting the people down.

Time after time, throughout the Old Testament, we read that the One True Living God, spoke to people. He spoke to those who 'knew' Him and to those who didn't.

Time after time we see the Living God turns lives upside down on those who deserved it and He opened the eyes of those who previously had not believed.

One thing that is sure though, once a person had an encounter with the Living God, no matter how they were before He spoke, they were never the same after He touched their lives.

God cannot lie, He cannot change who He is, was and will be. Depending on what lesson His people required as a reminder of who He was to them, be it, miracles, wonders, or a Truth to be witnessed or lived. Maybe something to be embraced and in some cases endured, God was and is true to His Word.

God's Holy Word is full of warnings and promises. It is full of love and understanding. Yet, we as His children continue to miss the mark. We continue to live in our own heads and we think we can always, 'deal with this tomorrow'. Yet because God cannot be untrue to His Word or promises, when the time comes, whether we are ready or not – our punishment or rewards will be received.

Numbers 23:19 (NLT) *God is not a man, so he does not lie. He is not human, so he does not change his mind. Has he ever spoken and failed to act? Has he ever promised and not carried it through?*

The most beautiful part of the Bible is all the chances God gives to His children. He continually opens the doors to yet another way for human beings to get close to Him.

So, as we close out the Old Testament and prepare to delve into the wonders of the New, remember that God loves you so much, that everything in His Word is to bring you close to Him. He wants you and me to be back with Him, the way He intended it to be.

God knew that there would come a time when He would have to make the ultimate sacrifice for the ones He loved. So next time you are trudging through the Old Testament and wondering what does it all mean, remember all this was to lead up to God bringing you back to Him.

How did He choose to do this?

He stepped down, and became one of us, He wanted to be part of us, He wanted us to realise He wasn't in the sky, distant, in a box, contained, or in a temple; separated.

He was flesh and blood who walked among them and felt their pain.

Yes, He is God in Flesh – Jesus.

Matthew 3:16
(NIV)

> 16 As soon as Jesus was baptized, he went up out of the water. At that moment heaven was opened, and he saw the Spirit of God descending like a dove and alighting on him.

As we closed out the Old Testament, I concluded that the whole of that part of God's Word was His way of preparing us for Christ and showing us His love.

Today's scripture, in my mind, is God handing the baton to Jesus and saying, 'Your turn – run with it. You know what has to be done and I AM with You.'

I am very emotional right now, as I have just this very moment, as writing this, had my own, I AM with you experience.

Allow me to set the scene. Many years ago, we were in a pretty tight financial situation and we were trying to determine if we could afford to move, our current lease was not going to be renewed. The rental market was tough and to find a place that suited us was pushing the boundaries way beyond what the budget added up to.

I was driving to work one morning, and I heard it so clear. "If I wanted to turn stones into currency I could. Do not be afraid, I will make a way."

This blew my mind, I was so awestruck, I told my family what I heard and, thus we trusted God and moved into the house. We, in all honesty have not looked back. It was like that moment was the turning point in our finances. We are not what the world would call rich, but, from where we have been in our past, we are loaded.

Now, to my *'are you serious God'* moment. The tears are still flowing, I must tell you.

I was reading through Matthew 3, as I do to prepare for these devotions. I try to grasp the fullness of what is happening, at the time, in God's Word, so I can try to do it justice.

I stumbled on Matthew 3:9 (NLT) *Don't just say to each other, 'We're safe, for we are descendants of Abraham.' That means nothing, for I tell you, God can create children of Abraham from these very stones.*

Mind Blown!

Let me try to explain.

All my life I have tried to do 'the right thing' I have stumbled a lot, but in essence, I have tried to live a good life. It meant and means zero really. A good life is not an eternal one. A good life or a history means nothing, until you have an encounter with the living God.

My 'stone' experience happened about 12 years ago. Today, this very morning, it has all fallen into context. God used His Word, His written, verified, truthful Word, to tell me that He is always with me! I felt sure and certain back then that God spoke. My life since that moment has proved it, but this, seeing this verse today, well that is a whole new deal. I am in awe. He gave me scripture I had never known existed, until this very moment, to let me know He is with me. Little old me!

So, here we are about to embark on the journey of the New Testament and straight out the gate, God is showing me, and thus you, He is here in us, with us, for us. He started the journey in Genesis, He brought it to life with the birth of Jesus, He carried it to a crescendo with the crucifixion of His Son and resurrection of Jesus – but He has left us with the greatest gift we could ever ask for. Himself, in Spirit, who dwells within us. Our very being is made up of God!

I am so excited right now, I can hardly wait to share with you the rest of the 3:16's that God has to share. I am renewed, energised and ready to serve my God with my whole heart.

Are you ready to do the same?!

Mark 3:16
(NIV)

16 These are the twelve he appointed: Simon (to whom he gave the name Peter),

Well God, you aren't giving me much to work with! These are the words that are presenting themselves in the forefront of my mind.

How many times have you said that? Or words similar, "That's not enough to do anything with!" Not just to God but to the people in our lives.

At this stage, when Jesus appointed the twelve, He hadn't been teaching for very long. He was still a new, exciting, thrilling healer. His Words were difficult to understand, and He referred to the scriptures in ways that scared some of the people.

Imagine if you will, you are living in the time of Jesus and He calls you – He calls you by name. Then, He changes your name! He says from now on, you will be called ….. *Who* has the authority to do that?!

You had grown up being taught that one day the Messiah would come, but honestly, did you expect it really? Especially to be called to walk alongside the Messiah – the Son of God – the Living God!!!

Simon, who became Peter was a fisherman – a nobody in the eyes of his peers. Yet Jesus saw something in him that no one else did. Jesus called him out and said, 'You are now mine, and to prove it, I will give you a new name. You are a new creation in Me.'

What was it, and, what is it, that causes people to change and follow Jesus? It's certainly not because it is easy. Easy to do or easy to understand. I think the Word of God is just as daunting to us today as it must have been to those who were trying to reconcile God in Flesh – that Jesus, a carpenter, from Nazareth, was / is the Living Son of God! As Mark 3 states, even Jesus' family thought he was crackers. By the way, the Bible does not use the word crackers.

I think people follow out of fear or love. Fear of what the person will do to them if they don't follow, or love of who the person is and the belief in them. Still, how many people in your life will you follow, through anything and everything, without question?

So, why follow Jesus? How do you choose to follow someone – possibly into death – without hesitation?

For me, I think it is that mankind tries to penetrate from the outside in, but God penetrates from the inside out.

We have the Holy Spirit who dwells within us (Romans 8). Not alongside, not outside, not off in the distance. He, who is God, dwells within our very being. If we go back to the garden, God reached in and Created us out of dirt, His breath, His very presence. He created us in "Our" own image – Father, Son, Holy Spirit. (Genesis 1:27)

Our very core, our very desire, whether we want to acknowledge it or not is to live our lives for our Creator – for we are a part of Him.

A child, who has had a rough time with their parents still wants to please them – why? DNA. We are a part of our parents, we are made up of them. We are genetically wired to love them, even if we hate them.

We are the DNA of God. Even if we want to turn from Him or never acknowledge Him, we can't help but have something missing if we don't love and live for Him. He dwells within us! Period, end of story, we cannot escape that.

So next time you are saying, "You're not giving me much to work with!" Remember that God has given you Everything to work with. He has given you Himself! And that, is more than enough!

Luke 3:16
(NIV)

16 John answered them all, "I baptize you with water. But one who is more powerful than I will come, the straps of whose sandals I am not worthy to untie. ~~He~~ will baptize you with the ~~Holy~~ Spirit and fire.

God woke me early this morning, earlier than the sunrise. I knew that meant He had something I needed to say for Him today. Yet here I sit at my computer, in the dark, reading today's passage and wondering, God how do I do this justice? How, as your humble servant, do I bring something to the table when the Author of the universe has already said it!

Then the tears start to flow. He is, in a tiny way, letting me see John the Baptist!

So, here I am for a moment, one of the greatest men in the Bible, one we have looked at and admired for his strength and his tenacity to speak about the One coming.

What a privilege, what an honour to be a called to introduce to the world the Creator, in Flesh!

I'm feeling overwhelmed at the thought of getting these verses wrong. I am confronted daily by my sinful behaviour, my bad attitude, language, irritation at things and people and I could write an entire book just on how far I fall short of God's Glory. Yet, for reasons I am unaware, He has chosen me to write these devotionals.

I wonder how John felt? Did he feel overwhelmed, did he doubt his ability, did he question, - *'really, me? I don't even wear proper clothes and I eat wild honey and bugs! Are you sure God, me?'*

Truth is, we are all called! We are all called to serve our God in some way. The words ministry, evangelism, preaching, teaching, missions and so on, scare the absolute willys out of me and probably a lot of Christians. We think we aren't good enough to do this, that or the other. We are just...... you fill the blanks.

I constantly doubt my ability to do these devotions, to share God's Holy Word. I doubt that anything I could say, either on paper or in person could have any profound impact on anyone. Then God reminds me – you don't! I Do!

I Do!

Such powerful Words when they come from the Creator of the Universe, the One True God who gave up everything to become flesh to walk among us. The One who has left us His Holy Spirit to dwell within us.

If I am prepared to allow God to work through me – how can I go wrong? If I am prepared to risk humiliation (that I said something daft, or did something less than), if I am prepared to stop long enough to allow God to speak, how can I go wrong!

It is not my words, it is not my actions, it is my obedience that God wants. It is my utter dependence on Him that He desires. Not that He is a control freak – He just knows best! He has created a path for my life – good, bad and at times really ugly. Yet I must praise Him for every single moment. For my life has been carefully, beautifully and wonderfully chosen to suit me! Little ol' me.

He has allowed obstacles to challenge me, almost break me and bring me to my knees. Why is it that some experience more heartache than others? Maybe we need to be brought to a place, so when the time is right we will step up as He calls.

A bit like those gaps in Jesus' life, we don't really know a great deal about John the Baptist either, other than, he was called, he answered and he did what God asked. Who knows what challenges he had experienced before he was ready?

We can say, yeah but his life was touched by God from conception. He was set aside, he was destined for great things.

Well, my friend, so were you!

Your conception, birth, childhood, and so on may not have made it into the greatest Works ever, but you were called to be for God. To be a light in this world for Him.

I often think of Esther and what she went through – she wasn't anyone special, not to mention she was a Jew. She was however, stunningly beautiful. This could have been seen as a bad thing when she was brought into the palace to become the king's play thing. God, though, took what the king had destined to defile and used it for His Glory. She was scared and didn't want to do what she was called to do. Yet, she heard the call, humbled herself before her God and acted.

Esther 4:14 NIV *"For if you remain silent at this time, relief and deliverance for the Jews will arise from another place, but you and your father's family will perish. And who knows but that you have come to your royal position for such a time as this?"*

The Bible is full of examples of everyday people stepping up when God calls. We are never privy to their walks prior to their calling, we are just shown, that even if they argued along the way, they stepped up in their humanness and did what God created them to be.

I argue with God all the time, I am totally convinced He has the wrong person for the job. Yet, I remain faithful and obedient and do what I feel He has called me to do. One foot in front of the other.

The first step is the hardest, yet the journey is well worth the effort! Step up, step out and trust!

John 3:16
(NIV)

> 16 For God so loved the world that he gave his one and only Son, that whoever believes in him shall not perish but have eternal life.

So, here we are, the best known 3:16 in the entire Bible. The most known passage in God's Word. This verse is the whole reason I believe I have been called to write these devotionals.

As Christians we have all read this verse, goodness, it is probably one of the few passages in the Bible we know off by heart. We know the Lord's prayer, but do we even know exactly which passage it is? Matthew 6:9-13 and Luke 11:2-4, in case you were wondering. When people are first introduced to Jesus, they are told of John 3:16. It is the foundation of our faith.

But, do we fully grasp the reality of what these words mean for us today?

I'm a mum! I think when you become a parent you can start to fully grasp the loving of someone so much that you would sacrifice yourself for them. I'm not trying to undermine other relationships, I just know that my selfishness was transformed to selflessness when my children were born.

Having adult children is painful. When they are hurting or going through trials, a simple I love you, a cuddle or a promise to 'fix it' doesn't really work anymore – it worked when they were little, but mum's magic formula doesn't work when the trials our children face are beyond our ability to fix.

When my children are going through 'adult' pains, my heart breaks for them. I want to fix things, I want to solve their problems. I want their pain to go away. Yet I am powerless to do anything, other than let them know I am here to talk to, cry to and comfort them. I can pray to the One who can do something, so that is what I do in my strength.

Now multiply that feeling of love for our children, beyond our comprehension, and we have the Love of God for each and every single human who has or will ever draw breath.

In John 3:16 God says He loved the world so much He gave us His Son! He fully knew what the world was going to do to His Son – to Him – yet He sent Jesus anyway. He fully knew that most of the world would turn their backs on Him, spit on Him, crucify Him, break Him (in flesh), and curse His very name. They would blame Him for everything that goes wrong in the world and forget to give thanks when things go right.

Yet, even in all this, He sent Jesus! Why?

Unconditional, unwavering, unbreakable, unchangeable LOVE!

Now I adore my children, but boy, over the years I have been so hurt, so angry, so frustrated I have wanted to pack it in and call it quits. I would get so angry with what they were doing, I would question if I was the right person for the job and if my love was enough. They were kids doing frustrating kid stuff, and yet some days my love was not pure.

God embraces His children - you, me, Hitler, Kim Jong-un, Putin, paedophiles, murderers, rapists, Mother Theresa, the most popular kid in school, the prettiest girl, the sexiest guy and on and on - with Love.

Pretty confronting, hey!

We would never put Charles Manson and Mother Theresa in the same sentence (sorry, just did) but God calls them both His children. He Loves them, they are His, regardless of whether they have chosen Him!

The thing about John 3:16 – God sent Jesus even though mankind would reject Him. He sent Jesus to us because He Loved us, not because we loved Him!

We love people in our life due to DNA or because they have done something that makes us love them. God sent Jesus even when we didn't love Him. The truth of John 3:16 is that God loves us, pure and simple, but the promise of John 3:16 is if we choose to love Him back then we will have everlasting life in eternity with God!

There are many passages in the Bible that talk about what our life can be like when we choose to walk with Jesus. These are tools to assist us with our walk after we have chosen to live in the

Love of God. Yet John 3:16 tells us in no uncertain terms that He offered us a path back to Him first! We didn't have to do anything. He made the choice to show us He loved us so much that He was prepared to take on the whole world's sin – from the beginning of time – yep all the way back to Adam and Eve's sin, and every sinful act that mankind has ever done since and that is ever to be. God, in flesh – took it upon Himself – so that we, as His children, can walk into eternity with Him.

Our part, is to choose!

Acts 3:16
(NLT)

16 "Through faith in the name of Jesus, this man was healed - and you know how crippled he was before. Faith in Jesus' name has healed him before your very eyes."

What is faith anyway?

Hebrews 11:1 *(NLT) 'Faith is the confidence that what we hope for will actually happen; it gives us assurance about things we cannot see.'*

Does that mean we don't need Jesus to have faith?

There are many people in the world that say they have faith. Many of these people don't know Jesus, they just have this sense that they must believe in something greater than what can be seen in front of them.

I've really been pondering this devotional, I have often wondered what real faith looks like. As a Christian you would think I have this down pat, but alas it is still my constant struggle.

So, today rather than try to answer this, I will share what I feel faith is. Maybe you will agree, maybe you won't. I hope either way it helps you on your journey.

I've learned that faith and fear are bitter enemies.

FEAR – **F**acing **E**xperiences that **A**ren't **R**eal!

The irony is, you have to have faith to have fear! Fear is really believing in something that hasn't happened yet. But from a negative perspective.

Faith is believing in something that hasn't happened yet from a positive perspective.

FAITH – **F**acing **A**ll **I**n **T**he **H**oly Spirit!

Let's turn our fear into faith. It is just changing the direction of the belief. Jesus is the only true way to do this. He wants what is best for us – always!

I've learned that faith is only a challenge when we are wanting what we want and not what God wants for us.

The Bible is full of scripture that talks about straight paths, directions, faith, asking in Jesus name, plans to prosper, knocking, seeking, finding. So why does stuff still go wrong and why do we rarely get what we want?

I think the key is 'what we want'. We live in a fallen world, things suck! It is what it is and because God loves us so much, He has allowed us to take the reins on our lives. He just asks that we turn towards Him and allow Him to show us the best path for our course.

We get caught up in what we want, we think we are letting Jesus lead, yet 99.99% of the time, we are saying, 'Lead me Jesus but turn right into Misery St ahead, I haven't quite finished bashing my head against that wall.'

I'm learning that faith comes from soaking in the scripture.

I am still working on this. My nature is very much – freak out first, have a meltdown, then take a deep breath and try to listen to what God is saying. I'd save myself so much grief if I skipped the first two steps.

My faith will reach its maturity when I realise, in every situation, that God really does have a path for me, I just don't need to drive. I need to learn to be chauffeured. This doesn't mean I do nothing in my life, it just means I jump in the vehicle that is heading in the direction God is leading and allow Him to take me there.

Life is not easy, in fact life can be really, really hard. Praise God that His Holy Word is full of scripture to help you through the tough times.

The more I read, embrace and live in God's Word, the more peace I have, even when things don't go my way. I am slowly, slowly learning that my way and God's way are very rarely the same. His way is so much better than anything I could ever imagine. The secret to true growth in Christ is when your plans and His plans align and you are at complete peace with it, and excited about the journey.

I've learnt that faith is not an excuse to get your own way.

Proverbs 16:9 (NIV) '*In their hearts humans plan their course, but the LORD establishes their steps.*'

I am almost fully on board with this verse now. I am learning not to ask so much, rather to give thanks, for the desires of my heart *and* to ask if they align with what God wants for me. I am an extremely anxious person, yet, more and more this anxiety holds less power over me as I surrender my *fear* to FAITH and give thanks for the outcome that God has already determined.

I've learnt that faith is not a once only thing, it is a journey.

Each new situation requires faith. We need faith in the little things, such as the historical things - each day the sun will rise and set. We need faith in the big things, the monumental things in our lives, the things that without faith will upend our lives. In these monumental situations, we have about as much control over the outcome, as we do about whether the sun will rise. Only our faith in what Christ will do will give us the victory to be overcomers.

We, as humans, have zero control over anything. Without faith, this is a really scary prospect. I am learning and rejoicing in this fact. I have no control – God does, and He wants my life to be a living testament to Him so that in all things, and I mean every wonderful, ugly, beautiful, detestable, amazing thing in my life, I give Him the Glory He deserves.

And finally, I have learnt that stepping out in faith is not stepping out alone.

When we move forward in faith, it means we are moving with the Creator of the universe right there with us. We don't have to face anything in our life alone. We are fully embraced by our Precious Saviour.

Where else would you want to be?

Romans 3:16
(NIV)

16 ruin and misery mark their ways,

Okay! That's a bit intense. Doesn't really leave room for anything happy and positive does it!

The good news though, this is writings from the Old Testament – pre-Jesus!

So why is it in the letter from Paul to the Romans?

Basically, the letter from Paul to the Roman church is to let them know that the in-fighting between Jews and Gentiles and even Jews to Jews must stop as we are all subject to God's law.

But!

When Jesus made the ultimate sacrifice of taking our sin to the cross he took every living being's sin to the cross. Not just the Jews!

Paul is trying to tell the Romans that we are all united in Christ

Jesus – end of story! If you are Jewish, then yes keep your traditions, but if you are Gentile then you don't have a history of rules to fall back on, so, it all comes down to your heart. Yet, if you are Jewish and only keep your rules and your heart is closed off to Jesus, then you are just as lost as any living person who has not received Christ as their Saviour.

Let's power forward to today – what relevance does the whole Jew / Gentile thing have for us today?

The answer is simple:

Every human who has a pulse has a chance to have an eternal relationship with Jesus Christ!

Booyah, drop the mike!

Who you are, where you have come from, your previous belief system, what crimes you have committed, what wrongs you have done, what god you have worshipped – this can be money, family, work, exercise, partner, or any god in the sense it is not the One True Living God! - no longer matters if you choose to follow Jesus with your whole heart.

Man's biggest argument about following Jesus is 'I am not good enough'. I will follow God when I am better, more financially secure, when I stop doing all the wrong things I do and so on.

Wrong! You will never be good enough to follow God!

Jesus, however, is! His sacrifice on the Cross – covered all that sin so you could come to Him dirty, shameful, broken, dishonest, disrespectful and any other horrid thing you can think of.

Jesus will change you from the inside out – we do not change from the outside in. We simply cannot change our nature. But Jesus can and does and will.

I used to look at 'holy' people and think I am so slack, I have nothing on them. God must love them more. What a load of crap! God loves me the same as anyone who has chosen to love Him.

Pure and simple - last word on the matter –

Ephesians 1:4-6 (NIV) *⁴For he chose us in him before the creation of the world to be holy and blameless in his sight. In love ⁵he predestined us for adoption to sonship through Jesus Christ, in accordance with his pleasure and will— ⁶to the praise of his glorious grace, which he has freely given us in the One he loves.*

1 Corinthians 3:16
(AMP)

16 Do you not know and understand that you [the church] are the temple of God, and that the Spirit of God dwells [permanently] in you [collectively and individually]?

When I thought that this verse was about looking after our body as it is a gift from God, that was hard enough. When I realised that the body that God talks about, is His Church, as in the unity of His people, that became super tough.

I'm not a people person. I fight within myself on a regular basis to get out there and meet people. I don't do small talk, I hate being put in a position where I have to socialise with people I don't know. I would rather spend my days in the safety of my four walls and not mix with humans at all.

I can do the look after the body part, got that down pat, but the other part – ummm, still a long way to go. I'm much more comfortable sharing God's Word from the safety of my desk, than to actually get out there and connect face to face.

Thankfully, God takes me where I am at. He is using the gifts He has given to do what He has called me to do.

Let's put our verse into context with the rest of the chapter. Paul is telling the Church of Corinth that they are still living in the world, doing worldly things, behaving like spoiled brats and not in unity with each other as the church is called to be. Sounds like the modern-day church, doesn't it?

Paul draws their attention to the fact that the church is saying they are apostles of himself or Apollos, instead of being apostles, (followers), of Jesus. Paul is trying to explain that Jesus is the reason as to why he and Apollos share what they share. In a nutshell, he is saying, if you are following followers, you can't be truly following Christ.

Paul is telling them that once you say you belong to Jesus Christ, you need to start acting like it.

I remember many years ago, I worked in the motorcycle industry. Yes, it is as loud, blokey and crass as you would think. I was right there amongst the bad language and bad behaviour, yet I proudly wore my cross necklace each and every day.

One day, I was serving a couple and they saw my necklace and commented, "Oh, are you a Christian?" I immediately placed my hand over my cross and said, "ah, um, yes, I am." They smiled and said that they were, too. Conversation over, they departed. But I felt empty. I realised right there in the midst of the world of motorcycles, I was not being a temple of God.

It was like God smacked me clean about the head with a bolt of lightning. I needed to let Jesus back into my life to be the centre of my being, so that there would be no question that I was a living vessel for Jesus.

I'd love to say that from that day forward I was a changed person and that I had a halo around my head and a neon sign saying *Jesus follower*. I am still a work in progress.

I've realised though, to be a temple of the living God, means that you reflect the one Whom you profess to serve.

Just as I work hard to keep my body healthy and happy, I need to work on my spiritual being to make God happy. Don't get me wrong, He loves me regardless of how I live my life, but He truly prefers that I show Him off to the best of my ability.

Showing God off to the world, is not as hard as you would think. It really is just living the life that you believe Jesus would have lived.

How do you find out how Jesus lived – read God's Word. Immerse yourself in His Holy Bible and you can't help but grow.

So next time you devour a dozen donuts in a sitting, or speak the wrong kind of words, remember you are a temple of the Living God and He deserves your absolute best. After all, He made you in His image – doesn't that deserve our respect?!

2 Corinthians 3:16
(NLT)

16But whenever someone turns to the Lord, the veil is taken away.

In my thinking, a veil is something to hide the face. A veil in today's world doesn't just have to be fabric it can be facial hair or make-up. Anything that covers the natural face, to transform it, to appear to be something else – in my view – is a veil.

Why do we wear veils? In weddings there are traditions – such as retaining the purity of the bride until she is revealed to the groom; or in some arranged marriages it was designed to cover the bride in case the groom wasn't impressed with what he saw – but alas too bad, by the time the veil came up, the deed is done.

In some cultures, a 'veil' is still worn by women every day. There are various stories as to where this originated. But, again, in my opinion it is a way to hide the woman from the world.

Over the years I have known many people who wear heavy make-up or cover their faces in facial hair because they don't like what they see, therefore, they can't imagine that anyone else would either. In an attempt to be more loveable, they change their face to suit the image they believe others will want to see.

There are others whose veils are behaviours, attitudes and even the persona they present to the world. All this is an attempt to hide who they really are.

In some ways, we all tend to wear a veil of some sort – we hide things from people we don't want them to see.

So, regarding the reference of the veil in this verse, it refers to Moses who after coming down from the mountain from collecting the 10 Commandments – the second time – his face was shining with the Glory of God – see Exodus 34. His shining face was too overwhelming, frightening and, dare I say, confronting, for the Israelites. Aaron, Moses' brother, suggested he wear a veil when he was with the people. In this case, it was not Moses wanting to hide from the people, it was the people wanting to hide from God.

In our current verse it is referring to the veil being something that separates us from the Truth of God's Word. It is like the veil not only covered Moses' face but also closed off the Word of God from entering the hearts of His people.

Paul is saying that when a person brings their heart to Jesus, that veil of division is removed. The person who receives Jesus as their Saviour sees the Word in all its Glory – there is no need to hide or be afraid. We are not bound by the law of Moses, we are set free in Jesus. Law locks us up, Jesus sets us free.

2 Corinthians 3:18(TLB) *But we Christians have no veil over our faces; we can be mirrors that brightly reflect the glory of the*

Lord. And as the Spirit of the Lord works within us, we become more and more like him.

Have you ever had one of those moments when something was revealed about someone and it is like the veil was pulled away and for the first time you saw that person for who they really are?

We see this often in romantic movies where the two protagonists don't really like each other, and then there is this 'moment' and all of a sudden it is like bolts of lightning, the sun comes out, the birds sing and everything is right with the world because, finally, the love of their life is standing right there in front of them and the world could not be a better place than right in this moment.

This, multiplied by a gazillion, is what it can be like when the veil is pulled away and you see Jesus for the first time.

Pull the veil, open your eyes and gaze into the loving face of Jesus. There you will find peace, love, joy and happiness like never before.

No longer will you need to hide behind your self-imposed prison of a veil of your own creation.

Jesus will make you a new creation and you will be set free.

Galatians 3:16
(NLT)

16God gave the promises to Abraham and his child. And notice that the Scripture doesn't say "to his children," as if it meant many descendants. Rather, it says "to his child"--and that, of course, means Christ.

Al was a young guy, about 15. He was a party boy, he liked the girls, he liked the fun and he also liked to get into trouble with the law – well maybe he didn't like it – but he seemed to do it well.

Al had made some friends with some Christian kids, he thought that they were cool, in a geeky kind of way, so he started to make his way to the local youth group.

He couldn't believe how welcoming everyone was. People picked him up to bring him to youth group, he made some real friends and started to feel as if he belonged. Everyone started to make him feel as if he was okay. That maybe he was loved. He didn't feel the need to hang with his troublesome friends as much. He wanted to hang with his Christian friends and learn 'Who' it was that made them the way they were. He started Bible study and he seemed to really want to make changes in his life. In his mind, for the first time in his life, he was accepted for he who was, not for what he did.

Sadly, this didn't last, not that the people stopped picking him up, or the kids stopped being his friends, it was that all of a sudden there were rules! It was like the Pastor decided, enough was enough, now you need to buckle down and do things the way the Church says you should.

It seemed love went out the window, and the law of the Church stepped in and so Al stepped out.

Al couldn't understand what happened. He had been trying to learn about a loving God and about a man named Jesus, who laid His life down for the whole world. For the first time, he wondered if that man, may have done that for him too. For the first time, through the Word of God and the actions of people around him, he felt, maybe, just maybe he could be loved as well.

Sometimes, as Christians, we get caught up in the law. We have rules, guidelines, regulations, dogma and the good old "well this is just the way we do it in our Church" mantra. Love, which is the first and foremost creed, principle and command of the Word of Jesus – often gets lost in translation.

Al was definitely accepted as who he was, in the eyes of Jesus. Unfortunately, the people of the church wanted Al to conform, stop hanging out with his troublesome friends, start coming to Sunday services, stop smoking, stop doing this, stop doing that and so on. Now, in principle, we may think that this is what is expected if he is going to become a Christian. But! We forget that Jesus walked among the unholy and never once tried to 'convert' them. He just lived by Who He was. Love!

Love changes us, not the law!

When Jesus came to set man free, He set us free from the law. This doesn't mean we get to break the laws of the land, it just means that we are loved, even if we do.

Jesus didn't try to Bible bash people, He walked with them, He taught them that God is love and even though the laws of Moses had had its place, those laws no longer applied. Jesus understood this most incredible, but simple fact.

If you love someone, you *want* to change so you reflect them!

Laws simply cease to exist, for you no longer need the bondage of them because you have chosen to follow the One who is pure, the One who breaks no rules, the One who doesn't run with the wrong crowd – yet is more comfortable eating with the lowest of low than with those who follow the law to the letter.

There really is something supernatural about Love. It changes a person from the inside out. We say a leopard can't change its spots, but love can. Out with the old, in with the new. The 'have to' change, becomes 'I want to' change. The old clothes are put away and the new robe of righteousness clothes you in a way you never knew possible.

Our verse today is Paul trying to let the Galatians know that God has been directing us towards Jesus since Abraham. God has been showing us His love since He created man in His own image.

Paul is trying to help the Galatians realise that the law is bondage and you will never be free by following the letter of the law.

May we all go forward and reflect the One we love. May we not be so caught up in the rules of the Church that we forget to love above all else. May our lives be a living testament to the One who gave it all so we could be free.

Ephesians 3:16
(NLT)

16 I pray that from his glorious, unlimited resources he will empower you with inner strength through his Spirit.

Square peg, round hole!

How many times in your life have you felt like that?

Everyone around you is fired up and excited about what is happening, and you feel as if you just don't belong but can't quite put your finger on why!

Yet, there are other times in your life when you are the one who is so excited about a project you can hardly contain yourself, and maybe others around you are wondering what you are on and if they can have some.

What makes the difference?

Conviction!

Something in you, at that time, for that purpose, is so strong that you can't help but share it, do it, profess it, embrace it, live it, breathe it. It is all encompassing – you think about it while you should be asleep, you are excited to start your day because you can get back to it. You put in long hours and it hardly feels as if any time has passed at all. You are driven by your cause. You are passionate about seeing it come to fruition. This, 'it', is the reason why you were placed on this earth.

When you are NOT convicted about something, you ARE a square peg in a round hole. You would rather be anywhere else than where you are right now.

Guilt can start to eat you up because everyone around you is excited and sees this 'it' as the thing that everyone should be excited about. Sometimes we try to fake it, we force ourselves to do the 'it' that everyone is doing. Eventually, we will burn out, get resentful and turn away.

How do we get conviction?

I believe that conviction is a God given seed that is planted within us and when He activates this seed to grow, nothing can stop it.

I remember a sermon I heard years ago, and it has had an incredible impact on my life. The pastor talked about crops, specifically a view of crops from an aerial perspective. Each paddock is separated, facing a different direction and growing something unique. It looks a patchwork quilt. He went on to say that each paddock is our life. We are to work our paddock – not the next one or the neighbour's or the one across the lake. We are to be a power of influence, to work our paddock and grow our 'seed' with conviction, passion and our whole being.

When you are working in the paddock that God has placed you, you are no longer the square peg, *you are the master gardener.*

Paul was telling the Ephesians that all people are one – there is no difference – we are all one in Christ.

This does not mean we have to all be the same. We all have our individuality and we can be a person of influence by allowing ourselves to be unique. The only way to do this, though, is to allow Jesus Christ to convict you. To fill you with His love and go out into the world and be a living, breathing, passionate example of His love.

Some people are passionate about animals. We can break this down even further by some being cat lovers, while others love dogs. Some are insanely crazy about saving insects and the critters that creep and crawl. While others are determined to save every furry furbaby from extinction.

Others don't really have a thing for animals at all and are called to far off lands to feed the hungry, yet others are called to feed the ones in their own neighbourhood.

God created us to be unique, to embrace our uniqueness and to be convicted in what it is we are called to do.

I fought the calling on my life. I tried all sorts of things to 'fit-in'. Not necessarily to what God called me to be, but with what the world thought I should be and I was miserable.

I didn't want to do these devotionals, I was scared. I didn't think I had anything of value to say. I thought what on earth can God do with me and my writing?

I realised it is not me – it is Him. I write what He tells me. He has just given me a gift to put it in a way that may resonate with some. I also realise, it may not resonate with others. That is why there are all sorts of people writing all sorts of things in all sorts of ways.

We are called to conviction; to be square pegs in square holes, or round pegs in round holes, or any other shape you can think of. If we are where we are meant to be, we just fit.

I love the Contemporary English Version of Ephesians 3:16:

God is wonderful and glorious. I pray that his Spirit will make you become strong followers...

Find your paddock, tend to your field and leave your neighbour to do theirs. When you are filled with the love of Christ and want to live according to His will and purpose for your life, nothing in this world will feel better.

Philippians 3:16 (AMP):

16 Only let us stay true to what we have already attained.

Paul is sharing with us in Philippians 3, that human satiation is fleeting and, in the big picture, has no purpose when it comes to pleasing God.

He talks about himself in that, if human success had anything to do with anything of value, he would be a champion. For in his time he did everything in accordance with the law.

When Jesus rocked his world, Paul came to realise that satisfying the flesh was a waste of time and energy. He may have had everything according to the world, yet he had nothing when it came to the real reason we are here.

Whether we like it or not, we are here on this earth to serve God. He created us for relationship. Mankind with all his exploits, discoveries and desire, seeks, above all things, connection.

When you do not know Jesus as your personal saviour, you seek this connection with whatever or whomever you can. In 100% of cases, eventually this 'connection' will leave you flat.

Sadly, over the years I have been to many funerals. Some, who have passed, have known Jesus and their funerals were such a celebration of life. Others have not known Jesus, but they have lived lives that have enriched others.

In these cases, these precious souls have tried to be the best version of themselves, trying to enrich the lives of others around them. In a sense they have *16 Stayed true to what they had already attained.*

Recently, I attended a funeral of someone who had not. His was a life of selfishness, bitterness, anger and, it appeared, disdain for every person who should have meant something to him.

There was no eulogy given by the family, just a chronological event of his life, and even then, only up to about 1974! The opening line, given by the Minister, was, "after his accident, 2010 – it seemed as if he lost his spirit and will to live!" After the funeral, it seemed as if there were no memories shared between the attendees. From what I could see it was a community who felt obliged to attend and then spent their afternoon sharing as if friends over coffee. The deceased was barely recognised.

Sadly, this was not a man who had stayed true to what he had attained. Or maybe he had, it was just not anything worthwhile.

I am sure that most of us would like to think upon our passing, the funeral would be attended by those who cared about us, wanted to celebrate our life and share memories of the way we had enriched their life. My heart breaks that this man died where, I am sure that, there won't be many who will really miss him. They may miss the impact he had on them, the abuse, shouting and disrespect. Yet they may find it hard to miss him.

As a follower of Jesus, I truly believe the only way to have a fulfilled life is to follow Him.

We need to let go of bitterness, before it digs into us so deeply, that is all anyone sees.

We need to release hatred, before that is all we have.

We need to embrace others, before others let go of us permanently.

We need to give up keeping score, before revenge, tit-for-tat and competitiveness are all we can do.

Life will always throw us curve balls. Life will give us heartache, pain, disappointment, and discomfort.

How we forget what lies behind, reach forward to what lies ahead and press on Phillipians 3:13-14 is a sign of true character. When we allow Jesus to be the driving force behind us, with us, and within us this journey becomes easier.

When we put our faith in the world, in material things and things of the flesh, we become disenchanted with the world and that is when hatred will fill us.

Seeking Christ first and foremost in our life is the only goal we should be attaining to. Then we need to stay true to this path. In doing so, we can have a full, loving, rich life where others will look at us and want what we have.

Colossians 3:16
(NIV)

16 Let the message of Christ dwell among you richly as you teach and admonish one another with all wisdom through psalms, hymns, and songs from the Spirit, singing to God with gratitude in your hearts.

She was an unlikely hero. Her life was one of disrepute, she entertained the men of the city to put food on the table. She followed along with the crowd worshipping who they worshipped, played by their rules. She was not what you would call a well-respected or honourable woman of the community.

What could a prostitute do to bring Glory to God?

I'm referring to Rahab the prostitute who hid the spies, whom Joshua had sent. These spies were to look for intel, as God had told the Israelites, to destroy Jericho. See Joshua 2-6.

Rahab's life was pretty dark. She worshipped idols. She was a Canaanite. She didn't really have any means to support herself other than to allow men to use her body. Her self-value must have slipped further and further away. Yet, we look a little deeper into the life of this hero and realise she was perceptive, intelligent and well informed of the goings on in her wicked city.

No matter what her life delivered, she certainly did not believe she would be called for anything higher in life than the lot she had already been given.

Then, one fateful night, two Israelite spies rocked up on her doorway.

She had a choice. Continue the path she was walking – or take a new direction.

Out of fear and reverence she decided to hide the two Israelite spies, sent by Joshua. Rahab knew the power of the Israelites and the God they served. It seems that she didn't hesitate to hide them, she was happy to misinform the King's men to protect them. All she asked in return, that when the time comes, she and her family be saved.

The spies agreed, but this did not come for free, she had to keep them a secret, place a red rope from the window so that the Israelites would know which house to save, have all her family in the house with her and then promise she would not turn on them later.

Not only did Rahab do what was asked, after the city of Jericho was destroyed, she went to live with the Israelites, married Salmon, from the tribe of Judah, went on to have a son, Boaz. Who grew to become the hubby of Ruth – thus making Joseph, Jesus's earthly father her direct descendant!

She made a choice!

She had heard about the Israelites' God and wanted to get some of this 'thing' for herself.

Maybe initially she did it out of straight up fear, maybe she saw her golden ticket out of there. Yet, to go on and live her life the way God intended could not have happened if she had not had a 'heart' change.

Rahab may have lived a long time before Jesus Christ, but God had a plan for her life – and as we see, she had a direct hand in Jesus's family line! Wow!

We look at the Holy Bible, as a whole, and from the very beginning to the very last Word – God is directing us towards Jesus.

Rahab, a prostitute, a woman of lowly standing, stood up, was accounted for and allowed the Word of God to dwell within her.

You may not be in the situation that Rahab was in. You just may not know which way to turn in your life.

I can assure you, the best decision you can ever make is to allow *the message of Christ dwell among you richly.*

As you grow in your faith, you will be able *to teach and admonish one another with all wisdom through psalms, hymns, and songs from the Spirit, singing to God with gratitude in your hearts. (Col 3:16)*

I can almost guarantee that, after her encounter with the spies, Rahab lived her life exactly as this verse says. God saved her from the life she had, wiped the slate clean and used her to fulfil the prophecy of Jesus's lineage.

May we be able to get out of our own way, stop focusing on

our 'now' and realise what our 'new' can be. To realise what an incredible God we serve and what a privilege it is to be called His.

Your past does not define your future. Your current choices are not the end of the world.

Let's live our lives to honour Him in all we say, think and do.

There is no 1 Thessalonians 3:16

2 Thessalonians 3:16
(NLT)

16 Now may the Lord of peace himself give you his peace at all times and in every situation. The Lord be with you all.

I grew up in Church. I am at least a fourth generation Christian. I have years of handed-down knowledge behind me. Personally, I gave my life to Christ when I was twelve at a *Youth for Christ* meeting. I walked to the stage in front of easily five or six thousand people. My mother is a lay preacher, my daughter valedictorian of Bible College. I have pedigree.

So, why, *oh why*, did I get it so wrong?

Maybe it was because the year following my personal encounter, my grandmother died before my eyes?

Maybe it was because my parents had to sell their business due to my dad's health; he spent what felt like a year, on the floor of our lounge in a brace for his back, unable to move.

Maybe it was because my cousin committed suicide before he

turned 21?

Maybe it was wrong choices, wrong relationships and so on?

Or maybe, just maybe I started to look *in* instead of *up*? Maybe it was because I stopped focusing on the Cross and started focusing on my own alter?

But I had pedigree! Shouldn't that count?!

Paul had pedigree! Look where that got him.

I may not have had the same intense, blinding experience that Paul had to shake him to the core (See Acts:1-19), but I had my own version.

In fact, my whole life was my version.

Every experience I have had in my life has somehow brought me closer to Christ. All the muddle and mess has only helped me to grow in my faith.

Every bad choice or every bad situation I have had in my life has helped me to grow to love Jesus more. I didn't see it at the time, but I look back now and see the adversity and choices were like being refined in the fire.

There is no growth without pain.

1 Peter 5:10 (ESL), *And after you have suffered a little while, the God of all grace, who has called you to his eternal glory in Christ, will himself restore, confirm, strengthen, and establish you.*

Jesus never left me, but I left Him. I thought that my pedigree, that is, the work my heritage had done, was enough. Paul writes in 2 Thessalonians 3 that we need to keep focused on Christ ourselves, we need to be a living example of Him. Our actions need to reflect our love, otherwise we end up where I ended up – looking at ourselves instead of the Creator.

My journey back to the Cross was and is a daily thing. I spend time with Jesus, I read God's Word, I absorb the Words spoken by Jesus and His followers. I seek out devotionals of godly people and I try to enrich my relationships with those who know Jesus.

It is only through constant relationship with Jesus, looking at Him instead of my situation that I can fully understand today's verse.

16 Now may the Lord of peace himself give you his peace at all times and in every situation. The Lord be with you all. 2 Thes 3:16.

Look at the words: the Lord of *peace himself* give you HIS peace! Not some peace, not a bit of peace, but his peace. He gives us HIMSELF – for He is peace! Not only does He give Himself, it is in every situation. Every means good, bad and ugly.

We don't always notice Jesus when things are good, but He is there. We do, though, notice His presence or our sense of absence when things suck.

It is only when we come to the place where we realise that Jesus *is* peace and He dwells within us at ALL times, that we know He is with us. We, then, can also feel He is with us in the horrid times.

I pray you come to a place where you know that Jesus is with you on the good days and you can feel Him in your daily walk. For when you know that Peace is with you in every situation, the dark days are still dark, yet there is a Light that radiates from within that nothing or no one else on Earth can offer. You still feel pain, heartache and anguish, yet there is comfort, for you know you are not alone. Bad things still happen, but somehow the Peace of Christ transcends our understanding and gives us hope.

Philippians 4:7 *(NLT) Then you will experience God's peace, which exceeds anything we can understand. His peace will guard your hearts and minds as you live in Christ Jesus.*

1 Timothy 3:16
(NLT)

16 Without question, this is the great mystery of our faith: Christ was revealed in a human body and vindicated by the Spirit. ~~He~~ was seen by angels and announced to the nations. ~~He~~ was believed in throughout the world and taken to heaven in glory.

The Holy Bible is a book of history, like you would find in any library or bookstore, yet it is the most argued book in history. Many scholars, over the centuries, have tried to disprove it but it seems to be an impossible task to do so.

Unlike any other book in history though, the Holy Bible is alive; it brings history to life in your very present. Yes, it was written for the audience of the day, and yes some of the things said seem strange to us. Sadly, a lot of the truest meanings of what the Bible is saying has been lost in translation. Man has tried, over the many centuries, to put the Bible in language we can understand. This unfortunately means that some of the beauty of the words have been watered down and we have lost the true depth of the relevance of this Living, Breathing Word in our every single moment. I am not a scholar, I am not trained in the Bible, I write these devotions based on what I believe God is giving me for the verse at hand.

I've said in previous devotions; and I reiterate now, the Holy Bible is a *love* story.

From the very first book, to the last, it is a documentation and a love letter from God to us. It is about showing us Jesus Christ, showing us how God wants to be a part of us, be within us, guide us, teach us, embrace us, uplift us and bring us peace beyond our wildest dreams.

I am as guilty as anyone of skimming over the readings in God's Word and missing the big picture.

When one goes to university or studies a subject, we don't just read the text book and all of a sudden know how to be a doctor, lawyer, mechanic, nurse, teacher and so on. We have to immerse ourselves into the subject, grab resources from everywhere and sit and listen to those who have gone before us to give us examples of how to be the chosen profession.

The Bible needs to be approached the same way.

We can't expect to get the Word of God by simply gleaning over it. Especially when it has been translated into a simpler language for us to understand. If we want to learn more, we need to immerse ourselves in His Word by learning from others who have gone before.

Why do we love Jesus?

As we immerse ourselves in God's Word, we start to see the pattern of Jesus woven throughout the scriptures. It is all about Him. When we start to join the dots and see how the Old Testament is a map towards the New, this is where we can start to form a relationship with Christ.

Quite simply, 1 John 4:19 (NIV), *We love because he first loved us.*

Why as Christians, do we serve this man?

People often say, "Why would you want to be a Christian? You have to change everything about yourself and give up everything that is fun!"

My reply often goes something like this:

I love my husband. In my love for him, I want to please him, so I have made alterations to my temperament to help make our relationship run smoother and to show him he is important enough for me to change some of my behaviours. I'm not saying that this has been easy or happened instantaneously, although some days, I bet he wished it had. But as my love has grown, my desire to be the best version I can be, for my husband, has grown too. When you love someone, you want to be the best version of yourself for them. If they love you, they don't force you to change, you *want* to change. The good news about loving Jesus, you don't have to do all the hard work of becoming a better version of you, He gives you everything you need, to be the best version of you, that you can be.

I love Jesus above and beyond anyone else. Because of this love, I want to please Him and serve Him according to what He has asked of me in His Word. Has this been easy? Ummmm, no!

But because of love, it is worth it.

God's Word, the Holy Bible, is a guideline of what is expected. This, in turn, is then a standard of how I am to treat all of God's children – that is you and me and every human who has ever drawn breath, in case you are wondering.

We serve God, because we love Him!

How does He differ to any other god that mankind serves?

God is real! He is the One True God and throughout history there is indisputable truth of the signs, wonders and miracles that God has 'shown-up' to prove His existence.

Mankind is cynical and there will always be sceptics. A person can see something right before their eyes and still deny. Yet, if you let the Living Word of God permeate into your heart, you will know without any doubt. God is God. We, who choose to love and serve the Creator of the universe, are not weak as some would say, but strong beyond measure. For the One who formed the very earth we stand upon stands with us.

When Paul was writing his letters to the churches, he was speaking from what he had seen. He was sharing in a language that was directed to the audience of the time. It was hard enough for people to believe in One True God then, it takes an incredible amount of faith to believe in God today. Today's verse is saying – this is what happened, this is how it happened and there is no doubt it happened and that is faith!

We argue today about faith – how can you believe in something you can't see – yet every moment of every day we believe in things we cannot see.

We believe there is wind, even if we can't see it; We believe the sun will rise and set, even though we cannot control it; We believe our food will grow, the power will come on, the internet will work and on and on it goes.

We have zero control over any of these things, yet we have faith they will happen. We have faith in things that man has done yet give no glory to the One who gave man the ability to do it.

When we, truly open our eyes to our world around us, we cannot deny God's love or His Truth. …. *"but the word of our God endures forever."* Isaiah 40:7 (NIV)

2 Timothy 3:16
(NIV)

6All Scripture is God-breathed and is useful for teaching, rebuking, correcting and training in righteousness,

When you are a child and you are at school, you tend to take what the teacher tells you at face value. The education system has had generations go before you, so therefore what your teacher says must be right. Right?

As you get older, you start to question how the teacher came to the answer and what is the purpose of all this learning? In science class, I was constantly being shut down by my teacher, as I kept asking, *why*? He didn't seem to know the answers, he just trusted the process and believed it to be true. Maybe a different teacher, with a different approach, might have helped me to find the answers I was seeking.

Since leaving school, I have studied in hospitality, administration, management, insurance, natural health and personal training. The one thing that has held steadfast, is my questioning of why!

Every aspect of learning needs to be backed up with another opinion. One person's interpretation of a subject may not be the same as someone else's. So, you need to get another opinion. Cross reference and learn how to understand the topic at hand in a way that resonates with you. Since I started learning about the human body, I have noted so many changes in opinion and research. Things that doctors and scientists have believed for years have been superseded. Things become clearer and the gaps are filled because brave scientists and, or doctors ask, *why?*

The Holy Bible is full of cross references and of people asking why. Many scholars, theologians, scientists and just everyday-people have tried, over the years, to disprove God's Word. Yet, it seems that when something is God-Breathed it is the only thing in this world that is truly infallible.

I have learned on this 3:16 journey, that some scripture is really hard to grasp. Some of it, simply, doesn't make sense and when you are not trained in ministry, it can be downright baffling.

Way back when I did the devotional on Judges 3:16, I discovered today's verse. It has been a solid reminder that even if I don't understand the relevance of a verse in the Bible, all scripture is God-Breathed and therefore has a purpose for us to learn from. My approach to verses and scripture that I don't understand? I learn! I ask questions of those who have gone before me. I read different authors and I read the Bible. I cross reference to ensure that the Word of God is being upheld in other writings.

When I studied natural health, I discovered there are a lot of opinions on spirituality. The Eastern religions have a very strong position in our natural health. Filtering what is true and godly as opposed to religious has been challenging. The one thing I have come to value is my wanting to "know more and know why".

If something doesn't sit well, I go back to the source. I go to the only thing in our entire history that has remained true and cannot be faulted. God's Word.

If something makes me feel icky inside, I cross reference to God's Word – for His Word cannot lie and cannot change. (Mal 3:6, Heb 13:8, James 1:17)

Today's verse excites me. It is so powerful. *All* scripture is God-Breathed, God inspired. Every word that is shared in the Holy Bible has the power of the Creator coursing through it. It cannot be wrong.

When you read the Holy Bible of God, and you don't understand a verse, check it with other books in the Bible. When a preacher shares the Word of God in Sunday service, that's what he is trying to do. Showing you the Old Testament is the forerunner and explainer of the New.

Did you know that the word honour is mentioned 147 times in the Bible? Love appears about 310 and truth about 235 times. Google a word that appears in the Bible and you will see just how many times it appears. This isn't because the writers couldn't think of another word. It is because they were concreting home the message.

We live in the age of endless opportunities to learn. You want to know an answer to a question, you search for it on the internet. This is so awesome. The trap is, though, that with that power comes responsibility and some people abuse that power. They just say what they have to say out there in cyber world. Very little factual evidence is used to support. A person can say anything, be anyone or profess whatever they like and the internet does very little to filter truth from fiction.

Yes, over the millennia mankind has tried and tried and tried to disprove, rebuke and argue with God's Word. Yet it simply cannot be done.

Don't be afraid to ask why. Don't be scared to get more answers. Feel free to search on the internet for whatever you like – but back it up.

I think the biggest gift we have been given is our gut instinct. When we tune into our intuition, it is really tuning into the presence of our Precious Father who is gently guiding us to the truth.

1 Peter:25 *(NLT) But the word of the Lord remains forever." And that word is the Good News that was preached to you.*

Hebrews 3:16
(AMP)

16 For who were they who heard and yet provoked Him [with rebellious acts]? Was it not all those who came out of Egypt led by Moses?

There are gods everywhere we look in our world. As a Christian, we often think that gods were a thing of the Old Testament, not overly of today. Yes, we have other religions who all think their god is the God, but I am more referring to all those things in our life that take a solid place in our lives, pushing out the One True God.

Let me name a few potential gods in our lives – money, work, health, sport, family, tv, our mobile phones, social media, friends, pets, cars, a single-minded pursuit of a goal. I hope you are getting the picture.

A god in our lives can be anyone or anything that takes our eyes, ears, minds, heart and very being, off God. The Creator of the Universe God!

Now, this gets a bit sticky, you see, because there are people out there who truly believe in God – well that's okay, Satan believes in God too. The issue is they don't believe in His Son Christ Jesus.

When God created the world, Adam and Eve walked in the garden with Him, they were able to walk, talk and fellowship with the Creator. Why? For at that time they were sinless and were able to look into the face of God.

Then they broke the rules and God's heart.

When God banished them from the garden, they, and the rest of mankind would never be able to look at God ever again. For God cannot look upon sin. It is simply impossible. The enormity of God is hard to comprehend but stick with me.

Ever since the fall of man, God has been trying to help us find our way back to Him. We can't look directly at Him, but we can have a stop-gap, until we meet Him in Heaven.

In the Old Testament, God used Moses to help His people 'see' Him. He then used high priests in the tabernacle who would sacrifice an animal as an offering to God. Throughout time, God gently came up with ways to help man get closer to Him again.

Humankind, being sinful, kept getting in their own way. So, God did the most amazing thing to show us just how much He loved us. He sent His Son to be the ultimate sacrifice for our sin.

We can't look upon God, for we are sinful, but Jesus, who is God in flesh, can look upon God, for they are One.

Jesus, who humbled Himself to become man, gave us a way to look at God, through Him.

Let's step back to the part where I said that even Satan believes in God. Anyone who believes in God, yet does not love Jesus, cannot have a relationship with God! When God sent Jesus, that was the final act, I guess you might say. Jesus was the crescendo, he was the final High Priest. No more sacrifices of animals, no more praying to the priests, no more throwing our sin onto the scape goat.

Jesus is the only way we can see God.

In short, if you don't believe in Jesus, you are really saying you don't believe in God.

Our puny little minds cannot grasp the enormity of God, we have tried over the millennia to put God in a box, to bring Him down to a size that we can make sense of, or control, you might say. But, let me ask you, what is the point of a God we can control?

I believe this is why we create our own little gods. It makes us feel superior, it is something we feel we can control.

If we are going to serve a God who created everything in this world, who sent Himself in flesh, so we could have a relationship with Him, don't we want Him to be bigger than anything we can comprehend? I know I do!

God often reflects the term tough-love. He cannot lie, cannot abide sin, cannot go back on His Word.

So, when we break the rules, the punishment is death!

Thank God for Jesus! Because of Jesus we get chance after chance to get our act together.

Jesus is the filter - we sin, it hits Him, He purifies it and then passes the purity through to God.

The people of Moses' day did not have the filter of Jesus, so they were left to wander aimlessly. A whole generation died before the next generation made it to the promised land.

Hebrews is trying to tell us, don't be like that! We have Jesus now. We don't need to wander aimlessly, we can keep coming back to Jesus, apologise for our behaviour and He continually purifies us before God.

God is Love and Jesus is the Way for God to bring us back home to Him where we belong.

Oh, by the way, footnote, or rather keynote – you are made in God's image. That means you are worthy and worth fighting for. He will never give up on you.

James 3:16
(NLT)

16 For wherever there is jealousy and selfish ambition, there you will find disorder and evil of every kind.

The calendar has just ticked over another year of September 11. One cannot help but reflect on that horrid day in 2001.

When I think of this day, I can recall where I was and the heartache I felt throughout the day as I thought about how many lost their lives and how many families would be forever affected by this tragic and evil day.

There have been countless theories and conspiracies over what really happened on this day, and I wonder if this is just man's way of trying to comprehend something that should never have happened. It is human nature to try and put a face to evil.

The simple truth of the matter is that day there was evil in the works and thousands of lives were ruined.

9/11 was astronomically devastating. We can point fingers and blame and curse and go on and on about the evil people who did this.

Let's bring it a bit closer to home.

Bullying in the playground, stealing office supplies from work, cheating on your partner, misleading the tax man on your return, filing a false claim, telling stories about someone, lying as to where you've been, and on and on we go.

Wait a minute Kerrilee, how can you put the evil act of 9/11 and cheating on your tax return in the same breath?

I don't, God does!

Dictionaries define sin as an immoral act that goes against divine law, in other words:

'a sin in the eyes of God'

We, as humans, put a grading system on sin and evil, but God doesn't. He just sees sin.

As much as I love this verse, it is very confronting. I've had jealousy and selfish ambition. I've told lies to cover up things I knew were wrong. Earlier in the book of James, he talks about the power of the tongue and how it can destroy everything, even though it is tiny.

Ever played Chinese Whispers? It is hilarious to watch a group of people go around a circle trying to recall and repeat the sentence that was given by the first person. The first and last sentence are so far apart, you have to wonder how.

That is the essence of gossip. A little flicker of a story and before you know it a bushfire has erupted, and the end story is nothing like the first.

Why do we spread stories about others?

Jealousy, one-upmanship, arrogance? Don't we really say things about others as a way of saying, *'Oh did you hear this, I would never do that, I am perfect.'*

I cringe when I watch a movie and it starts with a simple little omission and it just escalates to the point where, in some movies, every character ends up dead.

We think, ah it is just a movie, but, life has a way of imitating art and vice versa.

God is very clear on the punishment for sin.

Romans 6:23a(NLT) *For the wages of sin is death,...*

Thankfully He goes on to say,

Romans 6:23b(NLT) *but the free gift of God is eternal life through Christ Jesus our Lord.*

Read those two powerful little words – free gift.

As humans, we are going to sin, it is impossible for us not to as we are not perfect. We have faults and flaws and we can, sadly, be evil.

God knew this, when He decided to give us free will. He knew there was no way in all eternity that we could make our way back to Him without help.

So, He sent Jesus. The atonement for the entire world's sinful nature, from the beginning of the human race to the end.

The best part, Jesus did the work, we just have to accept this free gift of His love. It doesn't mean we will stop telling fibs or wanting to cut corners in life. It does mean though, that we will want to try harder not to do the wrong thing.

If you want this free gift, there is only one thing you need to do.

Romans 10:9 (NLT) *If you confess with your mouth that Jesus is Lord and believe in your heart that God raised him from the dead, you will be saved.*

How do you go about this?

Easy.

Feel free to use this prayer below and once you have spoken the words and felt the shift in your heart, Jesus does the rest.

Jesus,

I don't always do the right thing. I have lived my life according to my rules and my choices. I see that in reality, this has done me no favours. I want to live my life in a way that pleases You. You took my sin and misery to the cross and I can never repay you for that. What I can do though, is believe you did this for me. Jesus you are Lord, you died on the cross and You rose again to give me eternal life. Please forgive me for the life I have lived, and from today forward may I live in Your arms forever.

Amen.

1 Peter 3:16
(AMP)

16 And see to it that your conscience is entirely clear, so that every time you are slandered or falsely accused, those who attack or disparage your good behaviour in Christ will be shamed [by their own words].

She paid her fee, entered the bus and took her seat. Another day done, heading home to prepare the evening meal for her family. The bus was full that day and a man needed a seat. The driver declared that the row where she was sitting needed to be cleared so that the man could be seated. The three ladies sitting beside her moved. Rosa chose to stay put!

Rosa Parks, 42-year-old seamstress stood her ground. She was in her 'section' she had not violated any rules. By the laws of Montgomery, she was entitled to a seat in the 'black section' of the bus and, although it was preferred by white folk, the law did not say that she had to give up her seat to a white person.

Rosa knew she was in the right, but she didn't start screaming, or abusing the driver. She didn't strike out at the white man and call him names or insult his family. She didn't picket the bus or pull a knife or scream for human rights. She did precisely what she was entitled to do – she stayed seated.

Eventually she was arrested and removed from the bus. This is where the story could have ended. No one would remember her name, she would just be a side bar in the history of Montgomery and the rest of the world would be none the wiser.

But!

Rosa Parks was a woman of unquestioned honesty and integrity.

People attacked her, threw her in jail and tried to smear her name. Yet nothing could stick as she had nothing to hide.

This very act meant that the coloured community were able to stand their ground as well, leading to the introduction of someone we all know very well, Martin Luther King Jr, who become the MIA – Montgomery Improvement Association's, president and they boycotted the bus system on the day of Rosa's court appearance. Thus, setting into motion changes in equal rights. She went on to become known as the "mother of the civil rights movement"

How many of us believe we could stand our ground against such atrocities and be confident that no mud would stick if people started throwing it our way?

I hang my head, as I know I am not blameless. I honestly don't think I would have been as calm as Rosa. Rosa's whole life was blemished by racism, hatred, abuse and segregation. Enough was enough! Yet, she chose to take the peaceful way. Do the right thing yet remain strong in her conviction. She really was an outworking of our verse today.

Sadly, racism is still strong in our world today. We can leaf through the pages of history and see person after person remaining steadfast in their convictions to bring about change. Few are as peaceful as Rosa Parks, though.

Maybe you are going through something that you feel you are being unjustly 'segregated' for. Constant bullying at school, harassment at work, abuse from a partner, your work being plagiarised, the kids are off the rails, your family doesn't talk to you...... you fill in the rest.

How are you going to address this? Are you going to react, or respond? Abuse or speak calmly? Strike out or speak up? The choice is always yours.

When you know who you are, or better still, Whose you are – you don't have to go into these battles alone. Jesus is with you every step of the way.

Deuteronomy 31:6 (NLT) *"So be strong and courageous! Do not be afraid and do not panic before them. For the LORD your God will personally go ahead of you. He will neither fail you nor abandon you."*

Life is tough - Jesus is tougher. Life is cruel - Jesus is kind. We are broken - Jesus is whole. We say and do the wrong thing - Jesus is blameless.

I'm glad Jesus is in my corner and because of Him my past is swept away – *He has removed our sins as far from us as the east is from the west.* Psalm 103:12 (NLT)

We may not be blameless, but He is and that is all that matters!

2 Peter 3:16
(NLT)

16 speaking of these things in all of his letters. Some of his comments are hard to understand, and those who are ignorant and unstable have twisted his letters to mean something quite different, just as they do with other parts of Scripture. And this will result in their destruction.

John 1:1(NLT) *In the Beginning the Word already existed. The Word was with God, and the Word was God*

That's a truly powerful statement, don't you think!

In the Beginning!

Signifying that there was no before - the Word always was. It's hard to get your head around. Rest assured though, it should bring comfort, for if God has always been, then it means that everything else in the Bible is true also.

First thing, if God has always been, then He simply cannot be human.

So, if God has always been, then what He says about creating mankind is also true.

Again, this brings comfort for God is incorruptible, for corruption is a human failing.

God is also Jesus, for it clearly states that in the beginning the Word was with God and the Word was God. There are many scriptures, too many to list here, where we are confident, through God's Holy Word, that the Word is Jesus.

So, God is Jesus, Jesus is God. What of the Holy Spirit?

The answer to this one cannot be given in one simple scripture either. The Holy Bible is full of verses that lead to conclusion that God, Jesus and the Holy Spirit are three, yet they are One. I think my favourite verse is where Jesus tells His disciples that He will be ascending back to Heaven and wants to ensure that they can continue the work He has called them to do.

John 14:27(NIV) *Peace I leave with you; My peace I give you. I do not give to you as the world gives. Do not let your hearts be troubled and do not be afraid.*

Okay, so tying this all back to the verse at hand. Mankind, since the fall, has been trying to prove that there is more than one God. We have been trying to bring God down to our level, so we can control the situation or make sense of the what we cannot begin to comprehend. If our gods are statues then we can pick and choose if we 'hear' from them. If our gods are ourselves, well that just means we can do whatever we please, doesn't it? Problem with these theories of multi-gods is that the real, true Living God doesn't like to share us.

Exodus 20:5a (NLT) *You must not bow down to them or worship them, for I, the LORD your God, am a jealous God who will not tolerate your affection for any other gods.*

God has the right to be jealous – He created us. We are His and He knows what is best for us.

If mankind has been trying to disprove the existence of God, then it is super easy to dismiss the rest of the Holy Bible as well. If you don't believe all of it – then why bother believing some of it?

Our verse today is a warning – don't mess with God's Word.

In the Old Testament, Deuteronomy 4:2 (NIV), *Do not add to what I command you and do not subtract from it but keep the commands of the LORD your God that I give you.*

And the final book of the Bible, Revelation 22:18(NLT), *And I solemnly declare to everyone who hears the words of prophecy written in this book: If anyone adds anything to what is written here, God will add to that person the plagues described in this book.*

God is absolutely serious – His Word cannot be altered, changed, added to or subtracted from.

The Bible is the ultimate self-help book. We live according to His Word, we will have full life. We choose to mess with it, we deal with the consequences of our actions.

Think of it this way. There's a little ditty that can help you remember what God's Word is:

Basic **I**nstructions **B**efore **L**eaving **E**arth!

1 John 3:16
(NIV)

16 This is how we know what love is: Jesus Christ laid down his life for us. And we ought to lay down our lives for our brothers and sisters.

I find that John 3:16 and 1 John 3:16 say the same thing – Jesus loved us so much that He laid down His life for us – so that we could fully understand LOVE!

1 John 3:16 takes it a step further though – it states that we should be prepared to do the same!

Whoa, Nelly!

When Jesus came to earth to live among us, as one of us, He knew that ultimately His purpose was to take our sin to the cross. He knew that the end of His human life was death.

The end of our human life is also death. It is what we do with the dash inbetween birth and the end that makes the difference.

I've recently watched this documentary about how the Mob

came into existence. Wow! Talk about some seriously bad, bad people.

In all of the murder and mayhem of that time, I was consistently struck with the heart wrenching thought: these evil men were once innocent children. What went wrong?

What happened to turn children who once played with their friends in the streets, into men who killed for money, drugs, power and greed?

What happened to Cain and Abel? Two brothers who were raised by Adam and Eve. Cain killed his brother Abel out of jealousy! I really struggle to get my head around it.

How is it that a person can snuff out the life of another as if they are squishing a bug under foot?

Let me change gears for a moment.

Have you ever been in a pitch-black room? I mean where there is absolutely nothing but darkness.

I've been in dark rooms before. Scary darkness, but then my eyes adjust, and I start to see that there is a bit of light. There always seems to be a smidgen of light coming from somewhere.

My choice. I surrender to the darkness around me, or I focus and embrace the light.

John 8:12, ...*Jesus is the light of the world.*

When we focus on the light (Jesus) we are less inclined to act out what happens in the darkness.

Evil happens in the dark, because people don't want to be caught in the act of evil.

When we allow the light of Jesus to resonate within us and allow the wholeness of His purity to penetrate into our very being, we want to live as He lived.

Laying down our life for another, seems a bit overwhelming. Let's face it, none of us really want to die, just yet. We, as Christians know there is more on the other side of the grave, but honestly, most of us want to enjoy what we have on this side for as long as possible.

So, laying down our life for someone else seems to be a freaky option. I may be wrong, as I have not had to do it physically, but I think that if we were called to do so, I mean literally, we could – if we have allowed Jesus to be our centre. If pleasing Him and living for Him is our central focus.

I think this is what 1 John 3:16 is about – live our lives so that we reflect Jesus so much that if, physically or metaphorically, we had to lay our lives down for someone else, it would be as easy as breathing. We would do it without thinking.

Let us live our lives where our heart to serve Jesus is so strong, that the thought of dying for Him really is as easy as taking our next breath.

There is no 2 John 3:16, 3 John 3:16 or Jude 3:16

Revelation 3:16
(AMP)

6 So because you are lukewarm (spiritually useless), and neither hot nor cold, I will vomit you out of My mouth [rejecting you with disgust].

Have you ever been verbally slapped in the face by someone who loves you? Someone who cares so much that they are prepared to tell you something painful that you don't want to hear, so that you can change the path you are on.

I have! Ouch! It's like being jolted by a defibrillator – my heart stopped for a moment before I was jolted back to life.

I had a choice. I could rebuke the words of wisdom or I could embrace them.

As painful as it was to hear that I had flaws, (on numerous occasions) I have chosen to embrace the words, so I can grow and learn to be the person that my 'slapper' knows I can be.

In Revelation 3, Jesus is telling the churches of Sardis, Philadelphia and Laodicea that they are on a downward spiral and if they don't have a heart-start moment, they will reap the consequences of their choices. Eternity separated from Him.

With all the 'spirituality' and religions in our world today, Christianity is still the most uncool. If you are enlightened and spiritual, you are cool, but if you put a personal name to this enlightenment – such as the name of Jesus – the room suddenly goes quiet and no one quite knows where to look.

Now, I may be way off base here, but I truly believe those who are seeking 'spirituality' are more likely to find Jesus than those who 'know' of Jesus but are tepid in their beliefs.

Those seeking some sort of spiritual connection are at least cold (off-track, but passionate). God can work with enthusiasm. He can soften the heart towards Him to bring His child back into the fold.

Let me swing the other way, I also believe those who are full of angst and bitterness towards God for what man has done in His name, also stand a better chance of making it to heaven than those who are ho-hum about Jesus. Let's face it – hatred and love are on either end of the spectrum and one can easily be turned to the other.

It's a bit like the analogy, *it is easier to steer a moving vehicle.*

As Christians we have been given this gift of Life. We haven't had to work for it, like so many religions demand of their followers, and I think in some ways we become complacent. God warns us though, there is no place for complacency in His Kingdom.

When I felt that God had called me to write these devotions, I was scared. I felt unqualified and I didn't want to draw attention to myself. I kept getting little reminders that I really was meant to do this, but fear held me back. Then my very wise daughter told me, of course it is still my choice, but if God wants this written, then it will be written. If I chose not to, He would find someone who will. Did I really want to have God give this to someone else? Slap!

Instantly the words of Revelation 3:16 popped into my mind – the thought of being lukewarm for my God was unthinkable. Yet that is exactly what I was being.

The amazing thing about Grace and God's love is that it is never too late to turn towards Him. I wholeheartedly believe even in our dying breaths – God reaches out to us. "Are you going to remain lukewarm or are you going to come Home with Me?"

From Genesis to Revelation – God is showing us that He loves us and wants us to return to Him to live eternity in the Home He has prepared for us.

On this side of the grave, Christianity may not be for the cool kids, but trust me, Eternity with Jesus Christ is about as cool as it gets.

About the Author

Kerrilee Burkhardt is a writer and business owner, but her favorite roles are as a Mum and Noni.

She is passionate about the Word of God, and seeing people fall into His loving arms.

Kerrilee has written a children's book titled "Leapsneak: The Charlie Files" which can be found at all major online retailers.

She lives in beautiful Queensland, Australia.

www.ingramcontent.com/pod-product-compliance
Lightning Source LLC
Chambersburg PA
CBHW030255010526
44107CB00053B/1728